INTRODUCING SOUTHERN BAPTISTS

INTRODUCING SOUTHERN BAPTISTS

Their Faith
   &
Their Life

C. Brownlow Hastings

PAULIST PRESS   *New York/Ramsey*

Library of Congress
Catalog Card Number: 81-80052

ISBN: 0-8091-2364-9

Published by Paulist Press
545 Island Road, Ramsey, N. J. 07446

Printed and bound in the
United States of America

table of contents

foreword

In 1970 shortly after entering the work of helping Southern Baptists relate to their neighbors among Roman Catholics and Greek Orthodox I attended the National Liturgical Conference in Louisville, Kentucky. A Catholic priest and his lay associate spotted the badge revealing my Baptist connections. Immediately they challenged me, "We have always wanted to ask you Baptists one thing."

Thinking I was about to be questioned on some great Baptist distinctive, I inwardly prayed a quick appeal for wisdom.

"How do you get your people to tithe?"

"By the hardest!" I replied, somewhat limply. Since that day I have learned of many more questions that are beginning to be asked in both directions over the ancient barriers that have separated Catholics and Baptists. The most welcome openness of the Roman Catholic Church since the Second Vatican Council has given many of us undreamed of opportunities to engage in this kind of "interfaith witness" today.

In spite of much supposed prejudice on the part of people today against doctrine and theology, which are despised as being either impractical or divisive, many of us are finding that these kinds of questions persist. "Why do you Baptists believe ... ?" "What do you mean by ... ?" "Why do you do (or, more often, do not do) ... ?"

Thanks to a growing openness on the part of Baptists toward their neighbors of the Catholic and Orthodox faith there is much deeper relationship being established these days. And both groups are learning how to talk about the realities of their faith without much of the former spirit of denunciation.

To all those sincere friends who would like to learn more about those "peculiar people called Baptists," this book is addressed. It is designated "their faith and their life" because each derives from the other in the history of Baptists.

Also in characteristic Baptist fashion this is the view of one Baptist, reflecting his ideals and value judgments. So diverse are the people called Baptists that no single writer can do more than attempt a general viewpoint, colored by his own experiences. I am acutely aware of the limitation of this descriptive work to Southern Baptists, since the Baptists of the American Baptist Churches, the three large Black Baptist Conventions, and other Conventions as well have their own rich heritage to offer American Christianity. What is written here is intended as no disparagement of their worthy contributions to our common life in Christ.

In a work of this kind one tends to alternate between idealizing the realities and excusing the shortcomings. At times it may be apparent that I am preaching to myself and my own people. It is hoped that allowances may be made by the reader for all these limitations while the cause of mutual understanding is set forward apace.

The plan of the book begins with the experience of the individual Baptist in Part I, moves to the local church in Part II, and concludes with the larger relationships of the churches and the denomination in Part III. In order to make this available as a quick resource book, a number of appendices have been added concerning the social principles of the Christian Life Commission of the Southern Baptist Convention, a typical "Church Covenant" adopted by a local church. Two others comprise indices that hopefully will prove useful—a glossary of terms that are mostly unique to Baptists, and a listing upon the most frequently asked questions, arranged by major topics.

All Scripture quotations are from the 1901 edition of the American Standard Version unless otherwise indicated. "TEV" stands for "Today's English Version" published by the American Bible Society, 1971 edition. While it has been difficult to be consistent, when capitalized "Church" stands for the concept as a whole, "church" for a local congregation. Also whenever "Baptist" is used without qualifications, the reader is to understand "Southern Baptist" primarily.

Since I am not a qualified historian, I feel the inadequacies of the historical portions herein especially. On the matter of the controversies that have influenced Baptists I have chosen only those which have affected Baptist life in relation to Roman Catholics and other Protestant bodies. The interested reader is referred to the books quoted in the footnotes.

While this work is the product of years of teaching Baptists and others what Baptists believe, its writing awaited the opportunity of a study leave at the Institute for Ecumenical and Cultural Research, adjacent to St. John's University, Collegeville, Minnesota. This sabbatical in the fall of 1979 was made possible by the generous policies of the Southern Baptist Home Mission Board, Dr. William G. Tanner, Executive Secretary. I am grateful for the support of Dr. Robert Bilheimer, Director, Sister Delores Schuh, C.H.M., and Father Wilfred Theisen, O.S.B., of the staff of the Ecumenical Institute. The stimulating group of "fellows of the Institute" included Sister Kathleen Hughes, R.S.C.J., and a member of the International Commission on the English Liturgy (ICEL). Each of the nine scholars will be long remembered as loyal critics and friends.

My supervisors at the Home Mission Board, Glenn Igleheart, and Wendell Belew, have given constant support in this writing. I am particularly indebted to Claude Broach, past Director of the Ecumenical Institute of Wake Forest and Belmont Abbey colleges in North Carolina, and formerly pastor of the St. John's Baptist Church, Charlotte, for his careful criticism of both style and content of the manuscript. Father Thomas Stransky, immediate past president of the Paulist Fathers, and a member of the Baptist-Roman Catholic Scholars' Dialog, has made some helpful criticism. Father Joe O'Donnell, of the Glenmary Home Missioners, and Field Representative to Southern Baptists for the Bishops' Committee on Ecumenism and Interreligious Affairs, has been for three years my co-laborer and counterpart in Baptist-Catholic relations. He has so completely immersed himself in Baptist life that he knows more about us than most of us are willing to admit.

In these ten years many Catholic friends have contributed richly to my Christian worldview. I can only mention a few: three Glenmary priests who served as predecessors of Father O'Donnell—Frank Ruff, Robert Berson, and Will Steinbacher; the three Trappist monks of the Monastery of the Holy Ghost, Conyers, Georgia, who have for the past six years been faithful to a small group of Baptist ministers reading together the Greek New Testament once a month; Sister Jane Marie Richardson, of the Sisters of Loretto, in Kentucky, who has made a great contribution to the spiritual life of my wife and me through a long friendship; to both the Catholic and Baptist members of the Scholars' Dialog, who concluded their sixth session of the first series of theological discussions in the fall of 1980; and to Archbishop Thomas Donnellan, Bishop of Atlanta, who has been a faithful friend, even to giving a letter of commendation on my pamphlet, "Baptists and Catholics in Interfaith Marriage."

My wife, Jeanette, and our three sons and two daughters have believed in me and my calling to this "ministry of reconciliation of peoples," for which I am grateful. My secretary, Carol J. Phipps, has endured much tedious business during this writing.

I would like to add my thanks to Father Kevin Lynch, editor of Paulist Press, who first encouraged this work, and to Donald Brophy, associate editor, for shepherding it through its final gate. Also permission has been granted for the adaptation of my chapter, "A Baptist View of Authority" in *A Pope for All Christians*, Peter J. McCord, editor, published by Paulist Press, 1976, which has been used as Chapter One, "The Lordship of Christ."

part one

THE INDIVIDUAL IN RELATION TO HIS LORD

chapter one

THE LORDSHIP OF CHRIST

*A Baptist finds his
final authority in the
person of Jesus Christ*

Bishop Charles H. Helmsing in an address to a Catholic-Baptist Dialogue at Wake Forest University in 1973 was reminiscing about a conversation he once had with a notable Southern Baptist of his Kansas City diocese. President Truman was commenting at the table about his well-known penchant for an occasional social drink. The bishop recalled, "He referred to this at our conversation, and said to me, 'You know, the Baptists threatened to excommunicate me, but they couldn't. The only ones who could excommunicate me were my own congregation, and they wouldn't.' I learned then how Baptists understand *koinonia,* or fellowship, or community, or the local church better than if I had listened to a long lecture on the subject." The conversation turned later to Pope John's recent encyclical, *Pacem in terris,* which Truman warmly praised. The bishop concluded, "All of this made me realize that a Baptist, as a totally dedicated Christian, is formed in social action by free response to the Word of God, by personal meditation and prayer thereon, and by listening to commentaries of others on that Word, whether they be preachers or teachers."[1]

The good bishop has captured the essence of a Baptist view on authority. Baptists share with other Reformation descendants the primacy of the Scriptures as the external authority. They have a unique way of basing the inner light of the Spirit upon "the competency of the soul in religion" as the internal authority. And they are more willing today than ever to admit that such twofold authority operates within the arena of a fellowship of believers, whether that be defined as "what Baptists have historically believed" or "what I have always been told."

While the arena may condition the operation of authority, it can never be acknowledged as authoritative. While the inner light of the Spirit is essential to the understanding of the revelation God gives to man, such can never be reduced to an individualism or a mysticism that treats lightly God's revelation in history or ignores those who have a like spiritual endowment. While the Scriptures are the "final rule of faith and practice," they are only the means to the end of bringing the believer under the supreme Lordship of Christ.

It will be the thesis of this chapter, therefore, that the Baptist pattern of authority is dynamic and functional rather than static and abstract. While agreeing about the general pattern, Baptists will continue to disagree among themselves over the specifics of the pattern. According to changing pressures both from within and without the Baptist fellowship, they may now stress one or another pole of the pattern. Faced with any claims of hierarchical authority, they will emphasize the immediacy of their access to God through Christ alone. Confronted with critical doubts about the authenticity of the Bible, they may only take deeper refuge in "The Bible says," oblivious to any charge of circular reasoning. When asked by some to accept any list of "fundamentals of faith" as the touchstone of authority, they are likely to remind their overanxious brethren that "confessions are only guides in interpretation, having no authority over the conscience ... and are not to be used to hamper freedom of thought or investigation in other realms of life."[2] The viewpoint of this writer is from the position of one who has served his entire ministry within the fellowship of the Southern Baptist Convention. At no point should his remarks be taken as critical of other Baptist groups, nor does his ignorance of their writings intend any slight.

This kind of functional approach to authority is well illustrated by an experience of the writer. The deacons were painting the parsonage when he overheard one complaining to his partner of his stomach ailment. "You might heed Paul's injunction and

4

take a little wine for your stomach's sake," encouraged his partner.

Seeing an opportunity to show off his newfound learning in graduate seminary, the young pastor observed, "Brother White, did you know that verse is not in the oldest and best manuscripts of the New Testament?"

"It's in the oldest and best I got!" And he never missed a stroke of the brush. Deacon White's authority was functioning in a very practical way.

Another distinctive feature of this pattern of authority has to do with its locus of concern. Whereas most systems of authority have to do with *certitude* of the truth of religion, most Baptists are concerned with *assurance* in the experience of religion. Not, how can I be certain I am right, but, how can I be assured I am saved? This does not mean that the Baptist is unconcerned about the pursuit of truth. But suspicious of all claims by men, whether pope or scholar, church or philosophy, to encompass all of God's truth, he is content to order his priorities more modestly: "The Spirit himself beareth witness with our spirit, that we are children of God" (Rom. 8:16; all Scripture quotations are from the American Standard Version, 1901). Because of this inner witness he responds warmly to Paul's "for I know him whom I have believed, and I am persuaded that he is able to guard that which I have committed unto him against that day" (II Tim. 1:12).

Now there is nothing distinctive about the *fact* of the Lordship of Christ. Practically all Christians agree to the fact. It is the *way* that Lordship operates for the believer that makes the Baptist view unique. Ideally the Lordship of Christ is given as full and complete freedom to operate over the individual conscience as human frailty will permit. Every safeguard is taken to allow it to be undelegated, direct, experiential. In the final moment of decision, which may even be taken in concert with other believers, the soul stands naked before its Lord and cries, "What shall I do, Lord?" (Acts 22:10).

The very fact that the believer asks the question indicates that he is not deriving his authority from his reason or his conscience. It saves him from arrogant subjectivism. In finding the answer, however, the total man is involved: reason and conscience, memory and understanding, human wisdom and spiritual insight.

Now the average believer in the heat of decision-making is not all this analytical, but if he were, his reasoning might proceed something like this. "God, having of old time spoken unto the fathers in the prophets by divers portions and in divers manners, hath at the end of these days spoken unto us in his Son" (Heb. 1:1-2). "And the Word became flesh, and dwelt among us. . . . No man hath seen God at any time; the only-begotten Son, who is in the bosom of the Father, he hath declared him" (John 1:14, 18). Now the New Testament is a faithful record of those who were "eyewitnesses and ministers of the word" (Luke 1:2). As "inspired of God [it is] also profitable for teaching, for reproof, for correction, for instruction which is in righteousness: that the man of God may be complete, furnished completely unto every good work" (II Tim. 3:16-17).

If he is mature and well-taught he will draw upon the understandings of Scriptures both from those who have gone on before and those teachers in whom he has confidence. And Baptists perhaps more than any other major denomination have emphasized continuing Bible study for adults. It often seems like an end in itself or a flight into the first century, but it is ultimately directed toward that moment of truth when the soul needs to answer: "What shall I do, Lord?"

But he does not stop there, even with the finest interpretation of the Scriptures. He knows that as a believer under the New Covenant he has a promise that supersedes all claims to sacerdotal power: "I will put my laws into their mind, and on their heart also will I write them. . . . And they shall not teach every man his fellow-citizen, and every man his brother, saying, Know the Lord: For all shall know me, from the least to the greatest of them" (Heb. 8:10–11). He does not despise the gift of teaching, but he surrenders his mind and conscience to no teacher, pastor or friend, for he knows that he has the same open Bible and the same indwelling Spirit to give him light as they do. "And as for you, the anointing which ye received of him abideth in you, and ye need not that any one teach you; but as his anointing teacheth you concerning all things, and is true, and is no lie, and even as it taught you, ye abide in him" (I John 2:27; even concatenating Scripture references is characteristic of his style of reasoning.

6

Such is a very ancient method, going back to the lectionaries of the first Christian centuries).

Baptists, therefore, read each individual's privileges in the light of the New Covenant and the abiding presence of the Spirit. Believers are "sons of God" (Rom. 8:14), a "kingdom and priests" (Rev. 1:6), the "people of God" (I Peter 2:10). Since this is so, then all ecclesial structure must safeguard this freedom and nurture these privileges. Therefore, ecclesial authority is confined to the local church, which as the prime association of believers has the ultimate responsibility to each individual. Believers then associate together on the basis of a "church covenant." This is not a creed, which binds belief upon pain of excommunication. Nor is it a "confession of faith" which "constitutes a consensus of opinion of some Baptist body, large or small, for the general instruction and guidance of our own people and others concerning those articles of the Christian faith which are most surely held among us."[3] It is simply a pledge to support one another and the ministries of the church with Christian conduct and love.

Claude Broach has stated the implications of local church authority and autonomy:

> This group of believers acts freely, without constraint or supervision from any human authority, to order and govern its own life according to the New Testament. All decisions are made by vote of the congregation, with every member having equal standing and responsibility before God. Here are some of the things the local congregation must decide for itself:
> ——whom it wishes to ordain to the ministry;
> ——whom it wishes to choose as its pastor;
> ——whom it will elect as its deacons;
> ——how to operate its church school and total program of religious education;
> ——how to raise and disperse funds;
> ——how it will receive and care for its members;
> ——the order of service followed in public worship;
> ——committee structure to strengthen parish life and encourage participation in Christian service;
> ——extent of cooperation with other Baptist and Christian groups.[4]

7

Consequent to the principle of local church authority and autonomy, Baptists do not delegate any powers beyond the congregation. There is no such thing as "The Southern Baptist Church" beyond the Jones Street Baptist Church or the First Baptist Church of Anywhere. They can say, "The New Testament speaks also of the church as the body of Christ which includes all of the redeemed of all ages,"[5] but they do not conceive of its institutional expression beyond the local church. Consequently, Baptist associations, the first level of cooperation in missions, education, and benevolent work, state conventions, the Southern Baptist Convention and the Baptist World Alliance, are all made up of "messengers" from local churches, who constitute themselves an autonomous body for the purpose of carrying on ministries too difficult for a local congregation. There is no such thing as a Baptist "judicatory," as Truman pointed out. Most Baptists would not even relate the word ecclesially.

By and large Baptists have never been greatly impressed with the claims for or the search for a "true church." Most such movements, as, for example, Landmarkism, which arose in the nineteenth century and held to a kind of "baptismal succession" as the sign of the true church, have proved either divisive or inconsequential. Holding that the only conceptual "church" he has to deal with is the First Baptist Church on the square or the Jones Street Baptist Church, he is more aware of its human composition than of its divine nature. Its fellowship, ministries and worship are no less available to his highest dedication than to those whose Church is the means of their salvation or the continuing incarnation of their Lord. He is much more concerned with whether and how his church and denomination are carrying out the Great Commission than whether his local church is in all respects truly apostolic, holy, one and universal. His criteria are, therefore, very pragmatic: Is this particular church preaching the Bible? Are souls being saved? Is the fellowship warm and satisfying? What can they do for my children? Are they mission-minded? In this mobile age, if the answers to too many of these questions are weak or negative, he is not too disturbed, for he can always keep moving his affiliation.

So far we have approached a Baptist view of authority from the functional and practical standpoint. What do the theologians have to say?

Baptists have an inherited distrust of human reason, even reasoning about their faith. There is the anecdote about the preacher who took two hours with a highly reasoned sermon on the Proofs of the Existence of God. At the door one of his more pious members remonstrated: "Parson, in spite of your sermon I still believe in God!" She was enunciating a deep-ingrained feeling among Baptists: that the heart has its reasons one's mind can but dimly grasp. This does not mean that one reasons as far as he can, then takes a leap of faith into knowledge which is "out there in the dim unknown." Nor does it mean that faith is necessarily opposed to reason. It simply means in the mind of such humble believers that faith, which is more personal trust in the Lord than assent to a body of beliefs, is a more reliable way of knowing ultimate reality than is reason. To label this as "fideism" or "believerism" is to slander the witness of those who have experienced its end result: "peace with God through our Lord Jesus Christ" (Rom. 5:1). Their prayer for all men would be, "Now the God of hope fill you with all joy and peace in believing, that ye may abound in hope, in the power of the Holy Spirit" (Rom. 15:13).

Let us review briefly Baptist confessions of faith, with the limitations to these already pointed out. One of the earliest, which represents the thinking of the two groups of English Separatists in London and Amsterdam, out of which the earliest Baptists arose, is *A True Confession,* drawn up in 1595. Article 7 reads as follows:

> 7. That the rule of this knowledge, faith and obedience, concerning the worship and service of God and all other Christian duties, is not the opinions, devises, laws or constitutions of men, but the written word of the everlasting God, contained in the canonical books of the Old and New Testaments.[6]

One of the most complete statements of the authority of the Scriptures and of the need for inner illumination of the Spirit came from the London conference in 1689 of one hundred and seven Baptist churches. This *Second London Confession* was a rewriting of one originally issued in 1677 by a group of Baptists to show their general concurrence with the famous Westminster

Confession of 1646 (out of the Calvinist churches of England). It begins a long chapter on the Scriptures thus:

> 1. The Holy Scripture is the only sufficient, certain, and infallible rule of all saving Knowledge, Faith, and Obedience; although the light of Nature, and the works of Creation and Providence do so far manifest the goodness, wisdom and power of God, as to leave men unexcusable; yet they are not sufficient to give that knowledge of God and His will, which is necessary unto Salvation. . . .

> 5. We may be moved and induced by the testimony of the Church of God, to an high and reverent esteem of the Holy Scriptures; and the heavenliness of the matter, the efficacy of the Doctrine, and the Majesty of the stile [sic], the consent of all the parts . . . the full discovery it makes of the only way of man's salvation, and many other incomparable Excellencies . . . are arguments whereby it doth abundantly evidence itself to be the Word of God; yet, notwithstanding, our full persuasion, and assurance of the infallible truth, and divine authority thereof, is from the inward work of the Holy Spirit, bearing witness by and with the Word in our Hearts.[7]

These early Baptists did not trust the Church to pronounce with authority that the Scriptures were true, nor did they rely upon human reason to discern them to be the Word of God. Such requires that the Holy Spirit take the Scriptures and work within the mind and conscience this "full persuasion, and assurance of the infallible truth." Here is both the human and the divine at work, just as in the formation of the Scriptures. The human agency brings the Scriptures in the printed word and in the proclamation, which is both *witness*—"how shall they believe in him whom they have not heard? and how shall they hear without a preacher?" (Rom. 10:14b)—and *interpretation:* "Understandest thou what thou readest? And he said, How can I, except some one shall guide me?" (Acts 8:30–31). This human factor introduces the possibility of the misuse of the Scriptures. The latter are no proof against being short-circuited for the sake of humanly devised religious systems apart from the Lordship of Christ. Jesus warned his generation, "Ye search the Scriptures, because ye think that in them ye have eternal life; and these are they which bear witness of me; and ye will not come to me, that ye may have life" (John 5:39–40). Even the Scriptures can be perverted. Peter speaks of the writings of "our beloved brother Paul ... wherein are some things hard to be understood, which the ignorant and unsteadfast wrest, as they do also the other scriptures, unto their own destruction" (II Peter 3:15–16).

The divine Agent, the Holy Spirit, working both in the individual and in the community of believers, is therefore equally necessary with the Scriptures. He is "the Spirit of truth" who "shall guide you into all the truth: for he shall not speak from himself; but what things soever he shall hear, these shall he speak: and he shall declare unto you the things that are to come. He shall glorify me; for he shall take of mine, and shall declare it unto you" (John 16:13–14). So both of these—the Scriptures and the Spirit—lead unto Jesus and his Lordship.

The two most widely used confessions of faith in the last two hundred years have been the Philadelphia Confession of 1742 and the New Hampshire Confession of 1833. The wording of the New Hampshire Confession is practically unchanged in that adopted by the Southern Baptist Convention in 1925 and again in 1963:

> We believe the Holy Bible was written by men divinely inspired, and is a perfect treasure of heavenly instruction; that it has God for its author, salvation for its end, and truth, without any mixture of error, for its matter; that it reveals the principles by which God will judge us; and therefore is, and shall remain to the end of the world, the true center of Christian union, and the supreme standard by which all human conduct, creeds and opinions should be tried.[8]

While not exactly a confession of faith, a pamphlet entitled "Baptist Ideals" published by the Sunday School Board of the Southern Baptist Convention and drawn up in 1974 by a committee of eighteen, Ralph A. Herring, chairman, describes the three-fold pattern of authority. Its summary statements are as follows:

1. Christ as Lord. The ultimate source of authority is Jesus Christ the Lord, and every area of life is to be subject to his Lordship.
2. The Scriptures. The Bible as the inspired revelation of God's will and way, made full and complete in the life and teachings of Jesus Christ, is our authoritative rule of faith and practice.
3. The Holy Spirit. The Holy Spirit is God actively revealing himself and his will to man. He therefore interprets and confirms the voice of divine authority.

The ultimate unity and direction of movement of this pattern of authority is expressed in the closing paragraph on the Spirit: "The Spirit seeks to achieve God's will and purpose among men. He empowers Christians for the work of ministry and sanctifies and preserves the redeemed for the praise of Christ. He calls for a free and dynamic response to the Lordship of Christ and for a creative and faithful obedience to the Word of God."

From this can be seen the writer's emphasis that a Baptist view of authority is dynamic and functional. Nowhere is the end result seen as true or orthodox doctrines or beliefs, the true church, a rule or deposit of faith, or an infallible agent or agency. The moral and spiritual goal of submission to the Lordship of Christ, while always imperfectly realized under the human predicament, is obtainable practically without the agony of establishing finally those historically ecclesial issues.

It will surprise no one, Baptists least of all, that such a pattern of authority as we have described is susceptible to all kinds of stresses and strains. They will continue to argue among themselves and with the wider Christian community of scholars over all biblical issues, denominational polity, ecumenical participation, and spiritual movements. There will always be a conservative tendency to enforce confessions of faith, or some "fundamentals," as tests of orthodoxy. As churches and denominations grow and develop highly complex ministries with great financial outlays, the social forces that afflict all institutions

12

tempt individuals and groups to short-circuit the freedoms and the autonomy so long cherished.

The fundamentalist movement has sought to impose a theory of inspiration of the Bible based on claims of infallibility, literally interpreted. With their high regard for the Scriptures Baptists are particularly vulnerable. Hugh Wamble, professor of history, Midwestern Baptist Theological Seminary, Kansas City, has tried to maintain a balanced view:

> The Scripture's authority and infallibility relate to its supremacy as a rule for religious faith and practice. The official records of Baptists, prior to the twentieth century, do not claim that the Scripture's authority is dependent upon its historical accuracy or that it pertains to non-religious areas. There are some individuals, however, who assert that none of the Bible can be authoritative unless all of it is inerrant. Some self-styled Bible-lovers even suggest that it should be thrown away if it has one error. Quite frankly, it is hard to understand how anyone could treasure his theory about the Bible more than the Bible itself.[9]

Some Baptists will continue to insist on the "plenary verbal inspiration" producing an infallible Bible as being the sum of the Word of God. But even in their own interpretation and use, they do not carry through to the logical conclusion that every word is divinely dictated and on the same level of revelation. Clifton J. Allen, editor of *The Broadman Bible Commentary,* in his introductory article, "The Book of the Christian Faith," has pointed out the untenableness of such extremism: "Particularly, this view involves the problems of a divine will virtually imposed on the writers of the Scriptures, the submergence of the findings of critical studies as controverting full inspiration, and attributing to God attitudes and actions seemingly out of harmony with his revelation in Christ."[10]

The goal of religious authority as stated by E. Y. Mullins is worth repeating: "We stand for the free development of human personality, the complete unfolding of all man's power—intellectual, moral and spiritual—in short, for the perfection of man." Baptists believe that the final revelation of God which we have

13

in Jesus Christ is available to all men who may base their adventures of exploration safely there, for such is not the privileged possession of savants, scientists or sacerdotalists.

In closing his commentary on Jeremiah the writer has spoken of what it means to live under that "new covenant" the prophet foretold:

> The Church, then, is a fellowship of those who have a common experience—the forgiveness of sins; a common Master—who mediates the new covenant, which we commemorate at every Lord's Supper; a common Spirit— "who will guide you into all truth." These are the only valid reasons for having a congregational form of polity and operating on a democratic basis. Not that the majority is always right, not that *vox populi* is always *vox Dei*. But that the congregational polity is the only human guarantee that the Spirit of God has the freedom to speak the mind of God to the people of God.[11]

NOTES

1. J. William Angell, ed., *Catholics and Baptists in Ecumenical Dialogue* (The Ecumenical Institute of Wake Forest University, 1973), pp. 10-11.

2. Preamble to the report of the Committee on Statement of Baptist Faith and Message, adopted by the Southern Baptist Convention, May 9, 1963.

3. Preamble, *loc. cit.*

4. Claude U. Broach, *The Baptists* (New York: Paulist Press, 1967), pp. 16-17.

5. *The Baptist Faith and Message,* Article VI, adopted by the Southern Baptist Convention, 1963.

6. W. L. Lumpkin, *Baptist Confessions of Faith* (Philadelphia: The Judson Press, 1959), p. 84. Used by permission.

7. *Ibid.,* pp. 248 and 250.

8. *Ibid.,* pp. 361ff. I am indebted for this summary to the address of Dr. J. William Angell, professor of religion, Wake Forest University, to the Baptist-Catholic Dialogue of May 1973, entitled "Baptists and the Authority of the Scriptures."

9. Hugh Wamble, *Baptists, the Bible and Authority* (Foundations, July 1963, 6:212).

10. Clifton J. Allen, general ed., *The Broadman Bible Commentary* I (Nashville: Broadman Press), 1969, p. 8.

11. *Advanced Bible Study,* April-May-June 1971. Copyright 1971, The Sunday School Board of the Southern Baptist Convention. All rights reserved. Used by permission.

chapter two

THE COMPETENCY OF THE SOUL

*A Baptist believes himself to
be endowed by God to be
competent in all matters of
religion*

John Clarke was shocked at the persecution of
Anne Hutchinson, mother of fourteen and leader of a home Bible
fellowship, in Boston in 1638. He wrote in his diary:

> A year in this hotbed of religious tyranny is enough for
> me. I cannot bear to see men in these uttermost parts of
> the earth not able to bear with others in matters of con-
> science and live peaceable together. With so much land
> before us, I for one will turn aside, shake the dust of Bos-
> ton off my feet, and betake me to a new place. There I
> shall make a haven for all those who, like myself, are
> disgusted and sickened by the Puritan dictatorship. I
> shall make it a place where there will be full freedom
> of thought and religious conscience.[1]

Following Roger Williams' example, he moved to Providence
Plantation, purchased some land from the Indians and began a
second Rhode Island settlement which he named Newport. He
and his followers established the second Baptist congregation in
America after that of Williams in Providence.

These early champions of religious liberty did not wait for
State or Church to bestow freedom. With them it was an inalienable right beyond the jurisdiction of any societal powers. Indeed,

they believed it to be inherent in the dignity with which they were endowed by their Creator. Later Baptist thinkers came to call it "the competency of the soul."[2] This is related to the Reformation principle of "the priesthood of all believers." Baptists understand that principle to mean that each believer is his own priest in coming directly to God through Christ and dealing in all matters of faith and worship without the mediation of other beings or any religious rites. While this is a part of "soul competency" the latter is a broader concept. Competency has been well expressed in these words:

The individual, because he is created in the image of God, is responsible for his moral and religious decisions. He is competent under the leadership of the Holy Spirit to make his own response to God's call in the gospel of Christ, to commune with God, and to grow in the grace and knowledge of our Lord. With his competence is linked the responsiblity to seek the truth and, having found it, to act upon it and to share it with others. While there can properly be no coercion in religion, the Christian is never free to be neutral in matters of conscience and conviction.

Each person is competent under God to make his own moral and religious decisions and is responsible to God in all matters of moral and religious duty.[3]

There are three bases for this soul competency, all of which are endowments of God and innate to mankind under all conditions of life.

1. *Man is made in the image of God.* "Every individual is created in the image of God and therefore merits respect and consideration as a person of infinite dignity and worth."[4] Reformation doctrine teaches that while this divine image in man is marred, even ruined, by sin in all men, yet the image remains. We are still able to respond to God's Spirit. Even in the depths of the worst degradation we can still respond. The right of return is always open. The possibility of communication between sinful man and holy God is always available.

This is somewhat akin to what Roman Catholic theology teaches about "natural grace," that endowment which was not lost in the Fall of Adam and which informs the natural conscience of man apart from the revelation of Law and Gospel in the Scriptures. This may be what Paul refers to when he says, "For when Gentiles that have not the law do by nature the things of the law, these, not having the law, are the law unto themselves; in that they show the work of the law written in their hearts" (Rom. 2:14–15).

While reason and conscience are never a final guide for man in his relations with God, yet there is a natural wisdom, not limited to any race or religion, which reflects the image of God. This is the basis of man's responsibility to God that underlies Paul's judgment that all are "without excuse" (Rom. 1:18–23). But it is also the reason why we can never presume to ignore or condemn even the most ignorant or debased "heathen" (as we used to call them in our prideful exclusiveness). The *Imago Dei* still present in them demands our full respect for their human dignity, their consciences, and their right of self-determination in both religious and civil affairs.

2. Even though sinful, *we can be recreated* by God's saving work. The salvation provided in the Cross of Christ is available to all men without distinction. This is more than just cleaning up the original *Imago Dei* and restoring it to its function as practiced by Adam and Eve before the Fall. The goal of this saving work in us is that we might become "conformed to the image of his Son, that he might be the firstborn among many brethren" (Rom. 8:29b). We do not return to the innocence of Eden and the unformed character of Adam. We are destined as brothers of Christ to a greater end: "But we all, with unveiled face beholding as in a mirror the glory of the Lord, are transformed into the same image from glory to glory, even as from the Lord the Spirit" (II Cor. 3:18; the present tense of the verb, *transformed,* indicates that this is a process which is going on continuously in this life).

This saving work of God through Christ adds a new dimension to the competency already considered. Based on the eternal ministry of our High Priest, Jesus Christ, we have no need for any religious rites or intercessors to improve this competency. The author of Hebrews concludes that this gives us "boldness to enter into the holy place" (Heb. 10:19), and so he urges us to "draw near with boldness unto the throne of grace, that we may receive mercy, and may find grace to help us in time of need" (Heb. 4:16; the word *boldness* in these passages is derived from the word used of the Greek citizen exercising his right in the town assembly of "freedom of speaking").

3. The final basis of this competency of the soul in religion is derived from the fact that *the Holy Spirit lives within each believer:* "But ye are not in the flesh but in the Spirit, if so be that the Spirit of God dwelleth in you. But if any man hath not the Spirit of Christ, he is none of his" (Rom. 8:9). To have the Spirit of Christ certainly includes, but is much more than having, a like spirit. This is, indeed, the third person of the Trinity, the "comforter," sent by the Father who "shall teach you all things" (John 14:26). He is the one who awakens our conscience to wrong, guides us in moral and ethical decisions, and directs us toward truth (John 16:7–13). He speaks to our own spirits and confirms us in the family of God (Rom. 8:15–17). IIe is the source of life and power for the daily life of the believer. He is all the assistance we need in our prayer life: "And in like manner the Spirit also helpeth our infirmity: for we know not how to pray as we ought; but the Spirit himself maketh intercession for us with groanings which cannot be uttered; and he that searcheth the hearts knoweth what is the mind of the Spirit, because he maketh intercession for the saints according to the will of God" (Rom. 8:26–27).

The privilege of having the Spirit of God within the humblest believer was almost unthinkable to the disciples. Jesus promised the Spirit as God's gift (Luke 11:13). Peter explained to the crowd at Pentecost that the coming of the Spirit fulfilled the promise of Joel (2:28ff). The prophets had described the New Covenant relationship God would establish with his people. Ezekiel said, "A new heart also will I give you and a new spirit will I put within you. . . . And I will put my Spirit within you, and cause you to walk in my statutes, and ye shall keep mine ordinances, and do them" (Ezek. 36:26–27). The consequence of putting "my law in their inward parts" is that now there is an intimate, more reliable way of knowing the will of God. The Law of Moses was given through authoritarian teachers. Under the New Covenant such are no longer needed: "they shall teach no more every man his neighbor, and every man his brother, saying Know Jehovah; for they shall all know me, from the last of them unto the greatest of them" (Jer. 31:31–34; cf. Heb. 8:6–12). This does not do away with the role and function of Christian teachers, for the gift of teaching and its ministry in the Church is plainly evident (e.g., Eph. 4:11; Rom. 12:7). But this reality of the Spirit, available to every believer, does away with authorities who either officially interpret the Word or profess to bring a new revelation not available to the people otherwise.

A. WHAT KIND OF COMPETENCY IS THIS?

Negatively, this competency is not derived from one's righteousness, personal holiness, or pious practice. As one of the few absolutes of the Christian faith it cannot be improved nor can it be delegated by men or the Church. It is not negotiable, as though one could pay it out in return for some other value. It cannot be reduced by sin nor restored by repentance. Indeed, it is the only sure guarantee that forgiveness is directly available. The way "unto the throne of grace" (Heb. 4:16) has been permanently opened. If I am unaware of the way, or if I neglect to use it, this does not affect the reality of its existence.

Positively, then, competency is the divine gift to man by virtue of his nature as related to God. It derives from the Image and causes us to respond to the Creator and to acknowledge the Judge, even when we do not know his proper name. The very fact that God respects our competency grants us the status of free, moral beings. He runs the risk that we may rebel, deny our right, or sell our birthright of competency for a mess of security. Any kind of restraint upon this, any qualification of its absoluteness, therefore, destroys the moral value of its use. Any enforced doctrination denies the freedom of a human being to respond to or reject truth and love. These can only maintain their integrity through moral and spiritual suasion.

This is the basis Baptists rely upon for both individual freedom of conscience and religious freedom from the State.

Baptists cherish freedom of conscience and full freedom of religion for all persons. Man is free to accept or reject religion; to choose his faith; to preach and teach the truth as he sees it, always with due regard for the rights and convictions of others; to worship both privately and publicly; to invite others to share in services of worship and church activities; and to own property and all needed facilities with which to propagate his faith. Such religious liberty is cherished not as a privilege to be granted, denied, or merely tolerated—either by the state or by any religious body—but as a right under God.[5]

B. IN WHAT AREAS DOES THIS COMPETENCY OPERATE?

Since this is an inherent capability deriving from the Image, competency underlies the whole of man's existence. It does not make some individuals more capable than others in art or industry, philosophy or science, political or ethical expertise. It undergirds us by keeping open the way toward the ultimate realities of the universe and therefore making possible our rise to full human potential.

Especially does competency operate in religious experience. It makes possible the initial response of the sinner to the Holy Spirit as he draws us to God. The Spirit does not operate in a vacuum, nor apart from various means. He uses the Word of God, written and preached, the testimony of others, the situations and events of life. He is patient with slow responders and does not despise those understandings which are not yet pure or complete. He takes into account our cultural baggage and those unperceived social forces from which we are not yet liberated. As the divine Lover, he continues to woo the rebellious sinner long after human patience is exhausted. When the prodigal at last "comes to himself" in his repentance he discovers that the way back to the Father is already provided. The Father honors him by welcoming him in person, sending neither servant nor faithful son. Nor does he require acts of abasement or obedience. The heavenly Father deals with us directly at the point of our greatest need, the assurance of the divine acceptance.

Now Baptists, who have experienced this kind of open confrontation with their Lord, see no need for baptism or any other religious rite to facilitate what is prior reality. Having chosen their Lord freely and experienced the power of his forgiveness, they want no stand-ins to exercise faith in their behalf, not even their own devout parents. So they reject infant baptism because it deprives the individual the right to make the choice for himself. As some have put it, "God has no grandchildren." For others to make a commitment for the babe, even when it is expected that such will later be confirmed, compromises the moral responsibility of the child and denies his competency to engage the Lord for himself.

Because of this competency of the soul Baptists cherish the right of free access to God in prayer. Since this privilege has been given through the grace of God, it does not depend upon man's worthiness. The view of prayer that Jesus taught his disciples takes no account of any favoritism with God that anyone can win. There is always the human tendency to read into the character of God the standards of men. This results in holding that the more obedient and deserving are able to present their petitions more forcefully and so be rewarded more abundantly than those who are not. But this is to misunderstand the meaning of grace and make of it some kind of spiritual commodity which can be bargained for—a deep contradiction in terms. This intimate conversation between the child and his Father in prayer surpasses all human communication. Prayer, then, is cultivated as spontaneous, directed to any person of the godhead, and "from the heart" in order to be genuine. For these and other reasons Baptists do not pray to or through Mary and the saints. They feel no need to ask Mary to pray for them since they have experienced no problem in coming to God on their own account. And their jealousy for the role of Christ in personal experience makes them wary of placing any holy person too close to "the throne of grace." This might become a denial of their own competency and a threat to the undelegated Lordship of Christ.

A third area in which soul competency operates is that of reading and interpreting the Scriptures. Baptists recognize, of course, that the freedom of individual interpretation invites all kinds of error, but they are willing to take the risk of being wrong to preserve the freedom to find truth for themselves. And they have sufficient confidence in the unifying direction of the Spirit, who is the inner light of every believer, so that necessary agreement is possible. With the open Bible before those who are humble to the Spirit they believe that sufficient practical understanding of Scripture can be achieved so as to cooperate in the Gospel. This does not mean that disagreements and even divisions will not occur. These are seen as inevitable under the conditions of human frailty and sin which are still the lot of all in this life. At any rate, Baptists feel that agreement imposed by any lesser authority than the Word and the Spirit can only result in uniformity and are not true unity. Even when trusted pastors and teachers stand before them, they are mindful of the injunction, "Beloved, believe not every spirit, but prove the spirits, whether they are of God" (I John 4:1). They believe that the Spirit within the hearer is able to respond to the Spirit in the leader so that truth can be discerned.

What, then, saves this competency from rabid individualism? It must be confessed that pride and arrogance in some believers can produce just this extreme. But the more are saved from such a precipice by the recognition that no one lives a completely individual life in his religious experience. We are always in relation to others. We are never uninfluenced. We are indebted not only to those around us but also to those who have gone before us.

Josef Nordenhaug has provided the distinction we need:

> We must, I think, distinguish between individuality and individualism. Individuality contributes distinct values to the whole, while individualism disregards collective relationships. We must also distinguish *personal* faith from *private* faith. While faith in Jesus Christ is always personal, it is never private. Beyond the believer's concerns for his own life he must be concerned for his neighbor and the whole world.[6]

The community of the People of God develops a cumulative understanding of the mind and will of God that all must take into account. But both leaders and community must exercise care never to violate the competency of the person under these influences.

These influences must always be channeled through persuasion, by the evidence of the fruit of the Spirit. There is a harmony of the triumvirate of witnesses: the Word of God, the witness of the Christian community, and the inner light of the Holy Spirit. It is easy for us to yield our integrity and responsibility to some accepted authority: beloved pastor, honored teacher, influential book—even an edition of the Bible—respected parents or dynamic church. These all have their proper role of influence, but the final choice of belief and practice must be made in the secret of the soul's naked presence before God alone.

I may pray in corporate prayer or use a devotional prayer-book, but unless their words are truly *my* words, I have not engaged God for myself. I have only "said my prayers."

I may study the Bible under great teachers and share with devoted Christian friends, but I must finally judge what is truth, not because I find it agreeable to me, but because the inner witness of the Spirit convinces me.

I may profit by the testimony of another's experience in the Lord, but I do not need and cannot repeat his experience. I need my own.

This is something of what it means for a Baptist to speak of the competency of the soul under God.

NOTES

1. O. K. and Marjorie M. Armstrong, *The Indomitable Baptists* (Doubleday and Company, New York, 1967), p. 58.

2. E. Y. Mullins, *The Axioms of Religion.*

3. *Baptist Ideals* (Booklet published by the Sunday School Board, SBC, n.d.), p. 4.

4. *Ibid.*

5. *Ibid.*, pp. 4-5.

6. Josef Nordenhaug, "Baptists and a Regenerate Church Membership," *The Review and Expositor*, Vol. LX, Nov. 2, p. 141.

part two

THE FELLOWSHIP OF THE REDEEMED

chapter three

A BAPTIST UNDERSTANDING OF SALVATION

The basis of church membership

Another foundation stone in the building of the Baptist faith is frequently called "regenerate church membership." In distinction from those theologies which teach that one becomes a member of the church in order finally to receive God's salvation, Baptists teach that only those who have experienced regeneration, or "the new birth," are proper candidates for baptism and entrance into the church.

Since Jimmy Carter's frank statement during his first presidential campaign that he had been "born again," the Eastern media have kept the lines hot to various Baptist leaders asking what this means. They seemed largely oblivious to the fact that a great segment of American Christianity, usually called the evangelical wing, has proclaimed the necessity of the new birth throughout their history. With Charles Colson and other political figures speaking and writing on their similar experiences, the idea is not so startling anymore. Many charismatic Christians, who would have denied that they were ever other than true believers, began speaking of their renewal in the Holy Spirit as a new birth. In fact, the phrase has become abused by indiscriminate use in secular contexts. An over-the-hill baseball player suddenly has a great season and the sports writers talk of his being born-again. A political leader, whose Gallup Poll ratings were miserably low, makes a critical decision and suddenly he too becomes born-again.

A. WHAT IS THIS "NEW BIRTH"?

It should come as no surprise that the imperative, "Ye must be born again" has its origin in our Lord himself (John 3:3–8). Notable also is the fact that Jesus gave this command, not necessarily to the woman at the well, who was an obvious sinner (John 4), but to Nicodemus, one of the religious leaders of the people. The word *again* more properly means "from above." Jesus strengthens that by telling Nicodemus that this birth is "of the Spirit."

Most of the New Testament writers speak of this. James attributes the work to the Father: "Of his own will he brought us forth by the word of truth, that we should be a kind of first-fruits of his creatures" (James 1:18). Peter says that through "exceeding great promises . . . ye may become partakers of the divine nature" (II Peter 1:4). The Apostle John, in his characteristic way of linking love and sonship, says "everyone that loveth is begotten of God, and knoweth God" (I John 4:7). And Paul summarizes, "if any man is in Christ, he is a new creature: the old things are passed away; behold, they are become new" (II Cor. 5:17).

This is the work of the divine Spirit. But he does not impose this birth upon unconscious subjects. It only comes to those who want this new kind of life from above. Our wanting springs out of the sense of need in our sinfulness before God. The Spirit convicts or convinces us "in respect of sin, and of righteousness, and of judgment" (John 16:8). He then brings the good news of the Gospel to us and causes us to "turn around," which is the basic meaning of repentance, and place our trust in Jesus as Savior. We hear and respond to the invitation, "Whosoever shall call upon the name of the Lord shall be saved" (Rom. 10:14).

This is what we mean by "being converted." Baptists usually use this phrase in the passive sense, for we acknowledge that this is something which happens to us, albeit not without our conscious cooperation. The phrase is seldom used in the active sense of "converting" from one religious faith to a different one.

The primary theme of all evangelistic preaching for Baptists, therfore, is "Ye must be born again." All that is required of the sinner is that he acknowledge his sinfulness and in repentance toward God turn with faith to commit himself to Jesus as

Savior and Lord of his life. While this decision must be made at the center of one's being, it is expected he will, as soon as possible, "make his confession of faith" in the community of believers. If it is a private experience, it requires a public commitment. So Baptists do not take members into the church by private ceremony, but "upon public profession of faith." And this is most often in the context of the preaching of the Gospel. Here the Scripture links all of this together:

> The word is nigh thee, in thy mouth, and in thy heart: that is, the word of faith, which we preach: because if thou shalt confess with thy mouth Jesus as Lord, and shalt believe in thy heart that God raised him from the dead, thou shalt be saved: for with the heart man believeth unto salvation. For the scripture saith, Whosoever believeth on him shall not be put to shame. For there is no distinction between Jew and Greek: for the same Lord is Lord of all, and is rich unto all that call upon him: for, Whosoever shall call upon the name of the Lord shall be saved (Rom. 10:8–13).

It is on the basis of such promises as these that a Baptist can confidently assert "I know I have been saved." In saying this we do not boast in ourselves, nor in the uniqueness of our kind of experience, for we gladly acknowledge that this salvation is altogether the work of the Spirit through the grace of God and based upon the Cross and Resurrection of Christ. This is a present reality, which we believe every Christian can claim: "Beloved, *now* are we children of God, and it is not yet made manifest what we shall be" (I John 3:2). This does not allow us to take our salvation for granted nor deter us from seeking after the higher holiness. The next verse in John's epistle exhorts us, "And every one that hath this hope set on him purifieth himself, even as he [Christ] is pure" (I John 3:3).

The old Reformation battles over justification by faith versus justification by works still echo today. But however much one may hear Baptists ringing the changes on justification by faith alone, it must not be concluded that good works are ignored. They are seen, however, as the consequence, the fruit of salvation, and not the basis for one's acceptance with God. Paul puts faith and works in proper perspective: "for by grace have ye been saved through faith; and that not of yourselves, it is the gift of God; not of works, that no man should glory. For we are his workmanship, created in Christ Jesus for good works, which God afore prepared that we should walk in them" (Eph. 2:8–10).

Sometimes others challenge Baptists with Paul's statement, "Work out your own salvation with fear and trembling" (Phil. 2:12). We agree that we are called to work out into daily living that salvation which we have received. And the next verse explains why we have the desire and the power to do just that— "for it is God who worketh in you both to will and to work for his good pleasure" (Phil. 2:13).

There are two recent trends among Baptist interpreters that seek to balance the heavy Pauline emphasis in theology. One is a renewed focus upon the call of Jesus to discipleship. This has never been absent, but it can be neglected in the greater attention given to the divine element at work in our salvation. Also this shifts the focus of the goal of this saving work from what we humans get out of salvation to what the Lord, who does the saving, profits thereby (compare the parables of the Lost Coin, the Lost Sheep, and the Lost Son in Luke 15). It is for the purpose of his kingdom, his Church, his cosmic plan of reconciling all things and people unto himself that is the reason for our discipleship.

The other trend is a recovery of the sense of corporate responsibility in the Christian life, especially as it is lived in the Church, which is the body of Christ. As will be noted later, Baptists have little sense of responsibility to other Christians beyond that of their own congregation. They certainly shy from contemporary ecumenical movements. But it is fair to say that there is a growing concern to balance our strong sense of individualism with a wider sense of corporate responsiblity for all that portion of life with which God has entrusted us.

B. VARIETIES IN THE SALVATION EXPERIENCE

One of the most heartening features of the life of Jesus is his way of dealing with differing individuals each according to his peculiar nature. He has no standard approach, no uniform message. He always surprises us in his wisdom. For example, he tells the noble religious ruler, "You must be born again," but he discusses theology with the harlot of Jacob's well (John 3 and 4). We would tend to do just the reverse.

So is the way of the Spirit in the experience of salvation. Almost all who come to Christ will show certain commonalities: a sense of need because of sin, a turning away from self toward Christ, a commitment in trust to him as Savior and Lord, a sense of new being as a result. Each of these may show widely differing expression. Beyond these there is a profound mystery of the encounter of the whole person with Jesus Christ that cannot be defined or categorized.

Depending on age and maturity, there will be differences in the change in the moral life. Depending on the individual's sense of need prior to the experience, there will be differences in the focus of realization. Depending on the content of the Gospel message received, there will be different levels of understanding of what is happening. Depending on his rearing in a Christian home or in one of quite different religion, there will be little or great inner struggles over personal consequences of the decision.

The psychic element in the experience will depend upon many factors: age and temperament, moral condition of life prior to the experience, the immediate situation, kinds of friends and counselors involved. Since the whole person is involved, there will be the full range of response. The intellect accepts the basic truths of the Gospel. The will must decide to release one's life to the care and direction of Jesus Christ. The emotion is engaged in response to the divine love and then rejoices in the consequent peace and gratitude. The nature and intensity of emotion depends entirely upon the personality and has nothing to do with the genuineness of salvation. Now no one sets out to order his experience in precise stages or by rationalizing what he is doing. Like the man born blind whom Jesus healed, he cannot explain everything. He can only tell the one essential fact, "One thing I do know: I was blind, and now I see" (John 9:25).

Christians who assist in the birthing of this divine life in others will not try to force a standardized pattern of expression, either in words, emotions, or actions. The glory of the experience of Christ is that he enables the person for the first time to come into his true self and to be his own person with respect to all others. At the same time he takes on a new identity as "Christ's man," that is, a Christian.

Though these things be so, yet it must be sadly admitted that some immature Christians, even preachers, do not respect the Spirit's freedom nor the person's competency in trying to "bring people to Christ." Never guilty of using physical force to compel baptism, they are not above using psychological and other forms of manipulation, especially of children. This often results in giving the person a spurious experience which inoculates him against a genuine one later. And this adds "unregenerate members" to the church roll and sows the seed of internal troubles for years to come.

> In some instances children have been coaxed to make a profession of faith which they cannot in any fashion describe or defend. The invitation couched in terms of "Do you love Jesus? Do you want to follow him?" issued to a 6-year-old represents a genuine concern for a child's spiritual welfare; but the response elicited by such an invitation falls short of the promise and challenge of the Christian gospel. Happily, our pastors and teachers are becoming increasingly aware of the dangers of a superficial "conversion," which may actually hinder a responsible choice at a later time. Many Baptists have come to see that, in spite of our protests against infant baptism, we have been guilty of practicing it under the guise of believer's baptism in many instances of children's "conversion."[1]

But the risk is unavoidable. It can be minimized by careful recognition of the dangers and by developing a strong community of the Spirit in the congregation. In such a church the preaching and teaching of the Word and the disciplining of the fellowship can avail to reveal to such unregenerate members their true need of salvation. On the other hand, the rich variety of experience possible under this "way of salvation" more than offsets its risks. Herein is one of the glories of the Christian experience of salvation. It is capable of producing a veritable mosaic of beauty in the varieties of the people of God.

Baptists are often asked, "But what about the status of children? If they die before they are converted and baptized, are they lost?" Our understanding of individual responsiblity for sin and for one's relationship with God springs from the teaching of Jeremiah (31:19–20) and Ezekiel: "The soul that sinneth, it shall die: the son shall not bear the iniquity of the father, neither shall the father bear the iniquity of the son" (Ezek. 18:20). We acknowledge that everyone shares the race contamination usually called "original sin." But we do not find that guilt is thereby inherited in the light of the Scriptures above. Further, we believe that the total redemption provided in Christ takes care of infants and others who are not yet morally responsible for their own souls under God. We do not try to explain the status of infants who die. We simply take refuge in the goodness and wisdom of the Creator-redeemer: "Shall not the Judge of all the earth do right?" (Gen. 18.25). And Jesus reassures us that "it is not the will of your Father which is in heaven, that one of these little ones should perish" (Matt. 18:14).

In response to those who view baptism of infants as restoring "supernatural grace" and those who see it as bringing the child under the influence of the New Covenant, we reply that we see no need for such in the light of our view of salvation and the competency of the soul. No religious rite can effect a change in the divine-human relationship without the full participation of the human being involved.

On the other hand, Baptists are perhaps more concerned than many others to surround the child with Christian influences. The home is the first and strongest source of holy teaching and example. The Sunday School, starting with a "cradle roll department" and continuing through all ages, and other organizations in Christian training, music and mission activity, all combine to prepare the child for his moment of decision for Christ and the subsequent nurturing process. If we, then, are individualistic in our theory of conversion, we are highly corporate in our practice of Christian nurture. Baptists, along with many other Christian bodies today, are willing to take a hard look at all "plans of salvation." The ultimate question now becomes, "Does this way of making people Christian really produce disciples whom the Lord can use effectively throughout life?"

In all this discussion I realize that the reader may be

strengthened in the common view that Baptists are only concerned with the initial experience of salvation. It is true that this is the major theme of the proclamation of the Gospel to others. And Baptists feel that only a right beginning of the Christian journey can guarantee a happy ending. But we do teach a wider view of salvation. It *is* a lifelong work of the Spirit of God. It begins in the event of the new birth. It continues in the process often called "growth in grace" by which we are progressively made more usable to our Owner and more like our Elder Brother, Jesus Christ. It culminates at the Judgment, when our righteousness will be revealed in union with Christ (Col. 3:4) and the true worth of our service will be finally shown (I Cor. 4:4–5; for the future aspect of the saving work of Christ, see II Tim. 4:18; 1:12; 2:10).

C. THE CLAIM TO SECURITY OF THE BELIEVER

Most Baptists today believe that one of the greatest privileges they enjoy is the assurance of one's salvation. Historically, Baptists began with two streams running parallel, those influenced by the heritage of Augustine and Calvin, who taught that the "elect" will all finally be saved, and those who rejected that theology and majored on man's free will. These latter today are still represented by the Free Will Baptists in America. But most Baptists today would subscribe to the statement of faith adopted by the Southern Baptist Convention in 1963:

> All true believers endure to the end. Those whom God has accepted in Christ, and sanctified in His Spirit, will never fall away from the state of grace, but shall persevere to the end. Believers may fall into sin through neglect and temptation, whereby they grieve the Spirit, impair their graces and comforts, bring reproach on the cause of Christ, and temporal judgments on themselves, yet they shall be kept by the power of God through faith unto salvation.

When this is popularly expressed by "once saved, always saved," it unfortunately often leaves the impression that we are

34

boasting of our own righteousness or of some kind of infallible experience. We can be guilty of spiritual pride as readily as others, sad to say. But in our better moments we know that our assurance is not based upon the strength of our experience, nor upon any goodness we may have achieved. It is rather a testimony to our complete reliance upon the grace of God and his promises, upon the character and work of Christ for us, and upon the continuing presence of the Holy Spirit within us.

This is a gracious gift of the Spirit, a privilege which can be claimed through faith. Most of us recognize that one can be a true Christian and never claim this privilege, so we would not want to make such a test of fellowship. But we recognize great values for Christian life and service in this privilege of knowing that our ultimate salvation is assured through the promise of God himself.

We may look at this privilege in the light of Hebrews 10:23: "Let us hold on firmly to the hope we profess, because we can trust God to keep his promise."

This verse calls us to take up an attitude—"let us hold on"—based upon a reality—"we can trust God to keep his promise." This attitude becomes real when we come to grasp the fact that our hope is not a subjective wish or pious dream, but an unwavering reality. Now how can this be, seeing we are such fickle souls, plagued with such weak wills?

The author of Hebrews shows us that our hope is not anchored in our own wills, but in the character of God—"we can trust God to keep his promise." Our hope, then, is what God does in Jesus Christ:

> God wanted to make it very clear to those who were to receive what he promised that he would never change his purpose; so he added his vow to the promise. There are these two things, then, that cannot change and about which God cannot lie. So we who have found safety with him are greatly encouraged to hold firmly this hope as an anchor for our hearts. It is safe and sure, and goes through the curtain of the heavenly temple into the inner sanctuary (the Most Holy Place). Jesus has gone in there before us, on our behalf (Heb. 6:17–20, TEV).

35

Look again at the word of Jesus in John 6:37–40: "Everyone whom my Father gives me will come to me. I will never turn away anyone who comes to me, because I have come down from heaven to do the will of him who sent me, not my own will. He who sent me wants me to do this: that I should not lose any or all of those he has given me, but that I should raise them all to life on the last day" (TEV). So keeping us in secure relation with God is up to Jesus. He proves his obedience to the Father by working at our security. And this is not just some general saying that gathers up Christians as a whole. It is based on his personal and intimate knowledge of each one of us: "My sheep listen to my voice; I know them, and they follow me. I give them eternal life, and they shall never die: and no one can snatch them away from me. What my Father has given me is greater than all, and no one can snatch them away from the Father's care" (John 10:27–29, TEV).

Several times Paul uses the figure of *adoption* to describe our new relation with God through Jesus Christ. In Galatians 4:4–7 he says:

When the appointed time came, God sent his Son, born of a woman, born a subject of the Law, to redeem the subjects of the Law and to enable us to be adopted as sons. The proof that you are sons is that God has sent the Spirit of his Son into our hearts; the Spirit that cries, "Abba, Father," and it is this that makes you a son; you are not a slave any more; and if God has made you sons, then he has made you heir (*Jerusalem Bible*, Doubleday & Co., N.Y.)

So we are privileged to be adopted into God's family with all the rights of adult sons as heirs. We may use our civil laws to illustrate this reality. The laws of most states do not allow parents who adopt a child ever to disown or disinherit that child, as they can do with one born to them. When they adopt the child into their family, they take full responsibility for its past—its unknown heritage—its confused present condition, and its uncertain future.

And this is exactly what happens when we come to Jesus in faith and commit our lives to his keeping. All our past heritage of sins, our present confused and helpless condition, and our future destiny are his responsibility. Of course, I can cause problems in the family: I can disobey, I can dishonor the family name, I can fall short of realizing my full potential as heir. But his Spirit is at work in our lives to bring us back to obedience, to restore our reputation and to renew our purpose in life. Above all else, as Paul shows, his Spirit within us gives us this assurance by prompting us to call God, "Father, my Father" ("Abba" was the familiar word used by Jewish children as we use "Daddy").

Now what is the religious value of claiming this privilege of assurance? Just this, that we can once and for all time settle the matter of our eternal relation with God and get on with becoming what he has designed us to be and to do. As long as we are not settled about this, the center and focus of every religious act will be on ourselves. We will constantly be asking: What am I getting out of this? Am I doing enough to guarantee my salvation? Am I as good as others? And the reverse of this makes us critical and judgmental of other Christians. We compare ourselves causing detriment to each other. Guilt and fear are our constant motives in religion. Pride creeps in when we do manage to achieve beyond our fellow Christians.

Finally, assurance brings consolation in the loss of loved ones and peace in the face of our own death. We have a changed view of suffering. It is no longer God's way of punishing us so that we can become holy enough to live with him, but it becomes the occasion of entering into the Cross, the suffering of Christ in behalf of those who make themselves enemies of God. If we suffer for our own stupidity or as an "evil-doer," there is no merit, as Peter says (I Pet. 2:19–23), in taking such patiently, but there is always the open door to forgiveness (I John 1:9). But the spirit within the believer will make clear what suffering means, and we do not have to wallow in self-condemnation every time the common ills of life happen to us.

We have spent much time on the doctrine and experience of salvation as Baptists interpret it. If one is to understand "the people called Baptist," then the attention here is justified. The proclamation of and response to the Gospel to the end that all men everywhere might hear and believe constitute the heart and center of Baptist life. It is more fundamental than the Lord's Supper and baptism, even though our name was given us for the latter. It is considered the main function of the ministry, although pastoring is closely allied to it. Baptists may sound religiously chauvinistic when they periodically announce missions to "win the world to Christ," but they cannot do otherwise and be true to their sense of identity and purpose within the Kingdom of God. They might fight among themselves and split that which already was severed, but they are more apt to unite again around evangelism and missions than any other ecumenical banner grandly proposed.

NOTE

1. Brooks Hays and John E. Steely, *The Baptist Way of Life* (Prentice-Hall, 1963), p. 40.

chapter four

A BAPTIST VIEW OF
THE CHURCH

*A regenerate people who have
voluntarily entered into
covenant*

In the New Testament the term church designates God's
people in their totality or in local assembly. The church
is a fellowship of persons redeemed in Christ Jesus, divinely called, divinely created, and made one under the
sovereign rule of God. The church as a local body—an
organism indwelt by the Holy Spirit—is a fellowship of
baptized believers, voluntarily banded together for worship, study, mutual discipline, Christian service, and the
propagation of the gospel at home and abroad.[1]

The word translated "church" in the Greek New Testament,
ecclesia, means " called-out (or together) assembly." It was used
in the Greek version of the Old Testament for the congregation
of Israel. It was used in the Hellenistic world of that day for the
assembly of all free citizens in a city-state. This is what came to
be called in the Reformation a "gathered church" in contrast
with those territorial churches which operated on the basis of
cuius regio, eius religio, roughly meaning, whatever is the religion of the ruler, that will be the religion of his kingdom. It was
later known as a "free church" in that it had no ties with the
state.

The example of the way disciples were made and assembled
in churches in the Book of Acts indicates that one came into the

church after voluntarily accepting Jesus as the Lord and Savior and being drawn together by the Spirit. "Many of them believed his message and were baptized; about three thousand people were added to the group that day. . . . And every day the Lord added to their group those who were being saved" (Acts 2:41, 47, TEV). This produced a strong fellowship of believers who had a sense of interdependence and responsibility for each other.

It was not until much later when Christianity became the official religion of the Empire under Constantine that voluntarism in church membership gave way to the system whereby anyone born into a family living in a given area was made a member of the church by infant baptism. The Baptist insistence on its members having the new birth *prior* to being baptized is their chief ecclesial distinctive. For this their Anabaptist forbears were mercilessly persecuted by both Catholic authorities and Protestant reformers. They comprised the "third wing," the "radical Reformation." Out of this came their immediate insistence upon the right of individual conscience and the separation of the Church from the State. This led normally to a congregational form of church government, for if each member is endowed by the same Spirit through a common birth and all have the same privileges, then they concluded that no one can be ordained to rule over the whole.

Some define the essential marks of the church as "one, holy, catholic, and apostolic." Others locate the church where "the Word is truly proclaimed and the sacraments duly observed." Josef Nordenhaug gives the Baptist essential: "Without regenerate church members a church lacks the hallmark of the genuine church. The members in it must be in a living relationship to Jesus Christ."[2] So Baptists would tend to define the Church as people and what has happened to bring them together in Christ. They do not seek identity through creeds, or ordained hierarchy, or apostolic succession.

A. BECOMING A MEMBER OF A BAPTIST CHURCH

Baptists view the human experience as follows: one is born into a family and becomes a citizen of the state wherein he is born. As such he acquires family and citizenship responsiblities. By the new birth he is born into the Kingdom of God and as-

40

sumes responsiblity as a citizen of that Kingdom and as a child of God. By his free choice, then, he determines the will of God for his church membership and presents himself publicly before that congregation. He makes his "profession of faith" and asks for baptism and entrance into the fellowship of the church. The older practice was to require the one making profession of faith to stand before the congregation and "give his testimony" so that all would know of his conversion experience. In some countries, usually in mission fields, the candidate is required to enter a period of instruction lasting several weeks and then be examined by pastor and deacons before being baptized. A more lax practice in the United States assumes the candidate to have received sufficient instruction in the home, the church school, and by pastoral interview. When he then presents himself to the congregation, the church acts "to receive such a one as a candidate for baptism." The vote, having become less formal than before, now is more an affirmation of support and an acceptance on the part of the church to nurture the young Christian.

Once baptized, the church member may in due time "move his memberhsip by transfer of letter to another church of like faith and order." Originally this was not considered a "certificate of baptism" or of church membership that was the property of the member. It was a letter of commendation to a sister church, stating that the member was in good standing—that is, not having been excluded for due cause—and recommending reception by the new congregation.

Occasionally someone joins the church "by statement" that he has been a member of another Baptist church, which has since been disbanded and the records lost. Or, he may formerly have been a member of a Baptist church, then became a member of another denomination, and is now resuming his Baptist membership.

Baptist churches generally require baptism by immersion by a church "of like faith and order." When they ask one who has been baptized by another mode to be baptized by immersion, this is not to sit in judgment on the validity of his conversion experience. Since practically all communions consider the rite of baptism an initiation into the faith and life of the community, the church usually asks the believer coming from another denomination to accept the rite of immersion as a sign of full identification with this particular covenanted body. These traditional practices are not altogether uniform today, for Baptists also are experiencing some of the leveling influences in contemporary trends in American Christianity, especially in doctrinal discipline.

B. A BAPTIST CHURCH IS CONGREGATIONAL IN POLITY

On the recognition that the only authority over the church is Jesus Christ and in order to safeguard the competency of each believer, these Christians of like experience and faith come together in a covenant relationship to carry out the New Testament functions of a church. When a new church is "constituted," among other decisions a "Church Covenant" is adopted. This is not a creed in the sense of a minimum requirement of belief for entering and remaining in the membership. Nor is it a "confession of faith," which is drawn up by a church or group of churches in an association or convention. The latter spells out the beliefs held in common by a given body of Christians at a particular dated point of time. The covenant, on the other hand, is simply a brotherly agreement which pledges the members to mutual support, to a standard of behavior which reflects honor upon the body of Christ, and to an acknowledgement of responsibility for the support of the ministries and services the congregation seeks to fulfill. (See Appendix II.)

A confession of faith is also adopted at the time of constituting a new church. This is usually one which has been adopted by the association or convention with which the congregation intends to affiliate. Baptists do not accept such a confession of faith as authoritative except as the local congregation agrees to make it so for their own fellowship. Since the role of the confession of faith can be misunderstood or abused, it is important to give here a part of the preamble to the "Baptist Faith and Message" as adopted by the Southern Baptist Convention in session, 1963:

(1) That they constitute a consensus of opinion of some Baptist body, large or small, for the general instruction and guidance of our own people and others concerning those articles of the Christian faith which are most surely held among us. They are not intended to add anything to the simple conditions of salvation revealed in

the New Testament, viz., repentance towards God and faith in Jesus Christ as Saviour and Lord.

(2) That we do not regard them as complete statements of our faith, having any quality of finality or infallibility. As in the past so in the future Baptists should hold themselves free to revise their statements of faith as may seem to them wise and expedient at any time.

(3) That any group of Baptists, large or small, have the inherent right to draw up for themselves and publish to the world a confession of their faith whenever they may think it advisable to do so.

(4) That the sole authority for faith and practice among Baptists is the Scriptures of the Old and New Testaments. Confessions are only guides in interpretation, having no authority over the conscience.

(5) That they are statements of religious convictions, drawn from the Scriptures, and are not to be used to hamper freedom of thought or investigation in other realms of life.

Because there is one Lord over the church and because each member possesses the same competency of the soul, the logical form of church polity developed by Baptists is democratic. Every member is equal in rights, privileges, and obligations with every other member. This does not mean that there is not a division of the gifts of the Spirit, nor does it deny varying influence, but it does mean equality of privilege and rights. Among the members there will be many degrees of spiritual maturity, but the aid given the weak by the strong must always respect their integrity before God. Hence, leadership is based on persuasion in the Spirit and ability to inspire followship, and not upon authority of office or ordination.

The ultimate reason for democratic polity in the church is not because democracy is more efficient for it is generally less so. It is not necessarily more reliable, for the majority can surely be wrong at times. It is because this form allows the greatest freedom for the Holy Spirit to make his will known to the congregation and to provide for the continuing reform and revitalizing of the church. Baptists have experienced in the past much persecution or restriction of religious freedom in those countries where ecclesial control stifled the voice and will of the laity. Even within their own denomination their fear of clerical control has produced by-laws in most conventions that require a certain proportion of lay people to be elected to the boards and agencies of the convention.

It is possible, of course, under such polity for one man, pastor or lay person, or a small clique to lay hold on the church and control it. But sooner or later the Christian conscience of the people will rise up as they recall the words of Jesus, when his disciples argued over who should be the greatest, "The kings of this world have power over their people, and the rulers are called 'Friends of the People.' But this is not the way it is with you; rather, the greatest one among you must be like the youngest, and the leader must be like the servant" (Luke 22:25–26, TEV). Even Peter, the "chief of the apostles," appealed to his fellow-shepherds, "Do not try to rule over those who have been given into your care, but be examples to the flock" (I Peter 5:3, TEV).

On the other hand, under this polity it is also possible for the congregation to manifest such a stubborn spirit as to stifle the prophetic voice of the pastor and negate his leadership. The case of President Carter's home church in Plains, Georgia, is a good example of this. When blacks were refused admission to the membership, the majority of the congregation denied the leadership of the pastor and eventually forced his resignation. As often happens in such a situation, the minority felt they had no recourse but to withdraw and form a new Baptist church. But this does not always happen. A spiritual reversal on the part of the congregation and pastor together can often save the day. And it is always possible in this kind of polity for the Spirit to choose someone not previously in leadership in the congregation to lead the way to reconciliation and further progress.

There is an old saying among us, "Trust the Lord and tell the people." Baptist polity also calls for its reverse, "Trust the people and tell the Lord (in prayer)." Even though we know that a local church is a manifestation of the body of Christ, the

Church which the Lord guaranteed that "the gates of Hades shall not prevail against it" (Matt. 16:18), yet we also know it to be a very human society, subject to all the stresses and strains of any other. It is the arena for both the clash and the fusion of the divine-human encounter. It can on occasion know the shame of the one or the glory of the other. Here, then, is where faith, both in God and in man, is called forth. And if the local church fail and die, people are hurt and disappointed, but Baptists are realistic enough to know that the Kingdom of God does not stand or fall with any one particular manifestation of the body of Christ.

C. THE MISSION AND FUNCTION OF THE CHURCH

In its simplest self-understanding, the *ecclesia* (the New Testament word translated "church") is called out from the world to hear the Word of the Lord and develop its people and resources to enable them to return to the world as agents of the Kingdom of God. The church, then, is a function of and servant to the Kingdom; it is not to be equated with it.

The church has three functions which can be described as *centripetal:* (1) worship, when it centers itself upon its Lord; (2) fellowship, when it provides mutual support and discipline; (3) teaching and training, when through the pulpit and religious education it "maketh the increase of the body unto the building up of itself in love" (Eph. 4:16).

There are three functions which are *centrifugal:* (1) proclamation of the Word, which both brings people and societies under the divine judgment and announces the Good News of the divine redemption; (2) ministry, to all manner of human needs in the spirit and power of Christ; (3) mission, by establishing new outposts of the Kingdom for the propagation of itself in the world.

A congregation that tends to be strongly centripetal will become self-centered and soon die by the Lord's word, "He that loveth his life shall lose it." A congregation that tends to be only centrifugal will soon prove its emptiness, that it is all sound and movement signifying little. It will become loveless in its proclamation, disillusioned in ministry to an unappreciative world, and divisive in its effort to establish new churches. But a Spirit-guided balance of these opposite forces will produce a hundred-fold in Kingdom influence and power in their field of the world.

In carrying out this mandate from her Lord, the church will realize that it cannot serve the Kingdom alone. It will, therefore, enter into cooperation with other churches, both within its denomination and in the larger Christian community as the greater strategy of the Kingdom dictates. This we will discuss later.

D. THE OFFICERS OF A BAPTIST CHURCH

1. *The Pastor.* Baptists recognize only two officers in the New Testament: pastors and deacons. They understand the description of the pastor's function also under the other New Testament words, elder, bishop, and minister. Catholic and Protestant biblical scholars today agree the New Testament churches were very simple in their organization. Their "ministers" were more functional than official and usually drawn from their own fellowship. Even the distinction between clergy and laity was a later development after the apostolic age. Most agree now that arguments for ordination of different classes of ministers is for the most part a reading back into the New Testament of much later practices.

It should be apparent from the concept of the competency of the soul and the church as a regenerate people, in whom the Lord dwells through his Spirit, that the role of pastor in a Baptist church is primarily one of spiritual leadership. One way of describing the different aspects of his ministry is by means of the classic description of the functions of Christ: prophet, priest and king. Jesus said to all his disciples after his resurrection: "As the Father hath sent me, even so send I you" (John 20:21). Every believer has this basic three-fold role to play, but the pastor must both lead and equip his flock for this. If he is truly called of God, we believe that his gifts and calling will be apparent to the people of God. Paul speaks of Christ, "who 'gave gifts to men'; he appointed some to be apostles, others to be prophets, others to be evangelists, others to be pastors and teachers. He did this to prepare all God's people for the work of Christian service, to build up the body of Christ" (Eph. 4:11–12, TEV).

As prophet, then, the pastor proclaims the Good News in

preaching and calls men to decision in behalf of the Word which speaks to their consciences (II Tim. 4:1–2).

As priest, he ministers to the spiritual needs of the flock as their shepherd ("pastor") and leads them in worship. "The Christian priesthood finds its distinctive function, therefore, not in acting from God's side in the offering of sacrifices on man's behalf; it rather acts from man's side, as it leads men in faith to present their bodies a living sacrifice to God (Rom. 12:1)."[3] He teaches and trains in order that they may be equipped to fulfill their own "priesthood of believers" in the world (Eph. 4:11–12).

As king, he exercises leadership and provides discipline, not as "lording it over the flock," but as servant of all (I Peter 5:2-3). The motive power of this kind of kingship is redemptive love. The "rod and staff" of his shepherding (Ps. 23) is the Word, patiently and lovingly pressed on the flock. His authority is the evidence of the Holy Spirit speaking and working through him. The people respond by the discerning of the Spirit dwelling in them (I Cor. 2:13–15).

To qualify for this role, the pastor is expected to have experienced a calling of the Lord. This inner sense of divine call should be strong enough to commend him to the congregation of which he is a member. At his request and often on his testimony of a call publicly the church will vote to "license" him to the ministry. This is simply a letter of commendation to other churches stating that his own congregation believes in his Christian character and recognizes the potential of his divine calling.

With this calling there also come the gifts and endowments of the Spirit to enable his ministry. He is expected to "improve the gifts" by prayer, study of the Word and preaching and teaching whenever there is opportunity. Now more than ever, he is expected to pursue a full education, both in the liberal arts in a college or university and in the ministerial arts in a seminary. However, with their free polity and authority for ordination resting solely in a local church, Baptists have never been able to require education before ordination.

Usually during these days the young minister will take a wife and begin his family, for Baptists believe the marital experience helps to fit the pastor as leader and counselor to his people. Of course, this consumes time and diverts attention away from his ministry. But with the congregation sharing the larger function of ministry, the pastor is more and more looked upon as the leader and equipper for ministry. In early days and smaller churches the attitude all too often was "we pay you to do the work of the ministry; don't rely on us!" His wife, too, was looked upon as an unpaid associate pastor, or at least one who would busy herself in the music, education and women's work of the church. Today, more realistically the pastor's wife is given more freedom to assume the normal responsibilities of other church members.

Let us assume the one who has been licensed to preach is now in school. For his practical experience as well as his livelihood, he may preach before a congregation "in view of a call to be a pastor." If the church decides to call him, then they will also call for his ordination. This may be referred out of courtesy to his home church where he was baptized, or to the church where he is presently a member, or they may take the responsibility themselves.

The congregation that agrees to ordain him then issues a call to neighboring Baptist churches to send their ordained people—pastors and deacons—to form a "presbytery" for the purpose of examining the candidate and making recommendations (I Tim. 4:14). This calling of a presbytery is more than just seeking wise counsel. It is a recognition that upon his ordination the minister will go on to serve not only the church that has called him, but also the wider fellowship of Baptists through his continuing ministry for life.

The presbytery either privately or publicly (and sometimes both) will question the candidate on his "experience of grace" (his salvation), his sense of divine call, his basic Christian beliefs, his commitment to the Baptist faith and fellowship, and his vision of mission to the world. When the presbytery is satisfied, they recommend to the congregation that the "brother" be ordained. The congregation then votes their acceptance of this and instructs the presbytery to proceed with "the laying on of hands." After exhortations and a prayer of dedication, each member of the presbytery as well as sometimes other members of the congregation comes by the kneeling candidate and as he places both hands on his head he whispers a prayer or a word of support.

The rite of "laying on of hands" is usually not considered to

48

bestow the gift of the Spirit but only to publicly acknowledge that the Spirit has already evidenced his calling through the person's life and testimony. The rite, therefore, carries no sacramental powers or magisterial authority. Since all authority for religious rites and ordinances rests in the congregation, the call to become a pastor of a church carries with it the authority by the congregation to baptize and to administer the Lord's Supper. However, lacking a pastor, the congregation is free to appoint one of its own members or a visiting minister (or lay person) to lead in the observance of either ordinance. This ordination is considered to be for life, but upon grave cause it can be revoked only by the church where he is a member.

Today most Baptist churches extend an "open" call to their pastor. There are still several thousand small Southern Baptist churches that continue the former practice of an "annual call"—a kind of vote of confidence, or lacking such, a termination of the call. The congregation sets the financial support and any other guidelines for the functioning of its pastor and may review these from time to time.

When a church becomes pastorless, the congregation appoints a "pulpit" or "search" committee to seek out a new man. After considerable investigation and personal interviews with prospective pastors, the committee recommends and the congregation votes to call or to reject the recommendation and send the committee back for further search. In the change of pastorates both the man and the congregation try to discern the will of the Lord while taking into account many human factors and forces.

In all this discussion of the call and function of a minister, I have assumed the office of pastor to be filled by a man. For some time now churches are recognizing the proper ordination of persons to many different kinds of ministry—evangelists, missionaries, educators, chaplains, musicians, social workers, administrators and others. Further, a few churches have accepted women for ordination, usually for other types of ministry than the pastorate, but there are also a few women serving as pastors in some Baptist denominations.

2. *The Deacons.* The other office calling for ordination in a Baptist church is that of deacon. The New Testament pattern for this service is found in Acts 6:1–6. Seven men were appointed to a ministry of daily service (*diakonia*) to the widows of the con-

gregation so that the apostles could devote more time to prayer and the service (again, *diakonia*) of the Word. The moral and spiritual qualifications of deacons are given in I Tim. 3:8–13. In Romans 16:1, Phoebe, "our sister," is described as a deacon of the church in Cenchrea (*diakonos* in Greek is both masculine and feminine). Recognizing that the predominance of men in the church in New Testament times was the heritage from Judaism and reflected the mores of the day, some Baptist churches are beginning to ordain women to the diaconate.

Nowhere in the New Testament is the role of deacons described beyond a general ministry. Thus there has been wide flexibility in interpreting their work. An older generation of Baptists spoke of deacons as serving two tables—the table of the Lord, in serving the Lord's Supper, and the table of the pastor, in helping with the business affairs of the church. As churches grew large and complex there has been a tendency on the part of some to act like a "board of directors," even to requiring that all business of the church be approved by the deacons before being brought to the congregation. In recent times, however, there has been growing a greater emphasis upon the role of ministering to the needs of the congregation. Some churches divide the membership into groups and assign a deacon to serve as a kind of under-shepherd of his group. More and more churches are following patterns in business and government in assigning internal functions to committees that report regularly to the deacons and/or the congregation.

As in the case of pastors, deacons are examined for their qualifications and then ordained. This is for life, upon good Christian character, and the rite also includes the "laying on of hands" by a presbytery, usually drawn solely from the ministers and deacons of the ordaining church. But this does not mean that a church must appoint them to continuous service, nor that the church which they later join must use them on their "active list." Churches today are growing in their practice of electing deacons to serve for a definite period, usually three years, with the option of reelection to another term, after which they are assigned to an inactive list for at least one term before being reactivated. The diaconate is not considered a stepping-stone or a prerequisite to becoming a pastor.

The character and vision, the dedication and work displayed

by the group of deacons in a Baptist church can often have greater long-range influence upon the character of the church than any other factor. The pastor naturally sets the tone and provides the chief charism of leadership. Often the reputation of the church in the community and the denomination derives from him. But all of this goes for little unless he has the strong support and exemplary activity before the rest of the congregation of his deacons.

We have spoken of two ordained officers of a Baptist church. In the growing complexity of life and work in churches today much of the leadership will be done through lay people in Sunday School, training programs, the graded choirs, missionary and service organizations. To provide leadership and training to such a large number of lay people often requires a multiple staff of professionally trained ministers.

Here is the genius of much of the Baptist success. A large corps of lay people are continually being enlisted and trained for service in the congregation and for witness and ministry in the community beyond. The snare in all this, of course, is that the system can become so cumbersome that it consumes all its energies and resources in keeping the machinery going with little energy left over for the world outside.

E. THE CHURCH: GOD'S PEOPLE IN THEIR TOTALITY

It will be noted that our discussion of the Baptist faith has been moving from the individual to the corporate, from the smaller to the greater. So we have moved from the concept of the church as a local congregation to the Church as the universal body of Christ. Historically, however, the Baptist confessions of faith reversed the order. For example, the Second London Confession was drawn up in London in 1677 by a group of more than one hundred Particular Baptist churches (i.e., those Calvinistically-oriented who held to God's choice of "particular" individuals for salvation). This confession with few changes came to the United States and was adopted as the Philadelphia Confession of Faith, 1743, which for more than a century was the standard of Baptist churches. The London Article 26 on the Church reads as follows in the opening paragraph:

1. The Catholick [sic] or universal Church, which (with respect to internal work of the Spirit, and truth of grace) may be called invisible, consists of the whole number of the Elect, that have been, are, or shall be gathered into one, under Christ the head thereof; and is the spouse, the body, the fulness of him that filleth all in all.[4]

It is interesting that this concept of the Church universal dropped out of subsequent confessions, due largely to Landmark influence (see below, Part III), and was not restored until the 1963 confession adopted by the Southern Baptist Convention. Then Article 6 added to the main paragraphs on the church as local this statement: "The New Testament speaks also of the church as the body of Christ which includes all of the redeemed of all the ages."

One of the greatest theologians of the Church that Southern Baptists have produced was William O. Carver, professor of missions at Southern Baptist Theological Seminary, Louisville, during the mid-twentieth century. His chief contribution to biblical scholarship came in his commentary on Ephesians, *The Glory of God in the Christian Calling* (Broadman, 1949). In it he defined the Church, as found in Ephesians and Colossians, as "the spiritual Body of the Christ, constituted of all who are children of God through the calling of God and by their 'faith in the Lord Jesus.' This Church is conceived as organic with the Christ, his Body in the world, in the process of redemption, in the unfolding of history. In this sense, the Church is not organized, has no human head or headship. It is, as such and as a whole, no more concrete or visible than the Christ himself is concrete and visible in the sense world."[5]

It is into this Church that each believer of whatever Christian name is brought into the body of Christ by his salvation (not necessarily by the rite of baptism, as will be seen later). Carver elsewhere says, "Under the impulse of the Spirit, this member of the spiritual church voluntarily takes his place in the local fellowship and assumes his responsibility as a Christian in that church, for that local church is a concrete, organized expression of the one spiritual church."[6] So, then, one becomes a member of the Church as the body of Christ by the divine action and a member of the local church by his voluntary choice and commitment.

52

Over the Church no congregation, ordained person or hierarchy has any authority or control. Over the local body of believers who come together in covenant relation, the congregation accepts responsibility for the admission, nurture and discipline of each member.

Because Baptists have long endured persecution and restriction by a Church that claims authority over all citizens of a given state, they are exceedingly wary of any church which seeks to proclaim itself as the one, true church in universal, institutional form. Because of the nineteenth-century influence of Landmarkism, which taught that only through baptismal succession from the New Testament period could true local churches claim validity, Baptists are still divided over the proper distinction between the Church and the churches.

Another theologian has sought to harmonize these two concepts of the Church:

> *The* church is truly known only to faith, because it is constituted in and by the Holy Spirit. For this reason it may in one sense be described as invisible. But the church becomes visible in churches—in actual, visible, local companies. . . . The church is manifested and embodied in churches. . . . Its proper members are chosen by him, not by us. But the membership of local churches, which believers do control, must be determined by a sense of true churchmanship; i.e., churches must—so far as it is possible for us to make them so—be reflections and embodiments of God's church.[7]

Baptists generally have not bought the "branch theory" of the Church, i.e., that each church and denomination are but branches of the one Church. Russell Shedd makes it clear when he says, "The local church is neither a part nor a fraction, but the whole Church locally embodied."[8] Carver makes a strong plea for Baptists to make more of the whole Church: "In view of the biblical figure of the church as Christ's bride, the insistence of some that all uses of the term 'church' in the New Testament refer only to local organizations becomes absurd almost to the point of sacrilege, attributing to Christ a bride in every locality where a church is found. . . . How can one conceive of independent local bodies as growing into 'one holy temple of God in the Holy Spirit,' especially when the whole context of the paragraph [Eph. 2:19–22] emphasizes the unity of all members of the new human race produced by the cross of Christ?"[9]

The relevance of this struggle over the understanding of the Church in the churches will be seen again in our later discussion of the attitude of Baptists toward the ecumenical movement. It helps to explain also why Baptists will continue to live in the tension between their cherished freedom of the individual as expressed in an autonomous local church and their growing sense of responsibility for "God's people in their totality."

NOTES

1. *Baptist Ideals,* p. 8.

2. Josef Nordenhaug, "Baptists and a Regenerate Church Membership," *The Review and Expositor,* Vol. LX, No. 2, Spring, 1963.

3. Theron D. Price, "The Church," *Encyclopedia of Southern Baptists,* Vol. I (Nashville: Broadman, 1958), p. 274.

4. William L. Lumpkin, *Baptist Confessions of Faith,* rev. ed. (Valley Forge: The Judson Press, 1969), p. 285.

5. William O. Carver, *The Glory of God in the Christian Calling* (Nashville: Broadman, 1949), p. 31.

6. William O. Carver, "Introduction," *What Is the Church?,* Duke K. McCall, ed. (Nashville: Broadman, 1958), p. 7.

7. Theron D. Price, *op. cit.,* p. 276.

8. Russell P. Shedd, *Man in Community* (Grand Rapids: Eerdmans, 1964), p. 135.

9. Carver, "Introduction," *op. cit.,* p. 8.

chapter five

THE SYMBOLISM
OF THE ORDINANCES

*The community's rites
as witness and worship*

Baptists speak of baptism and the Lord's Supper as "ordinances" rather than sacraments. By this we understand that Jesus gave orders to his disciples to observe only two. Jesus told his little band just before returning to the Father: "Go ye therefore, and make disciples of all the nations, baptizing them into the name of the Father and of the Son and of the Holy Spirit: teaching them to observe all things whatsoever I commanded you" (Matt. 28:19–20). Paul reported that at the founding of the Supper Jesus told them, "Do this in remembrance of me" (I Cor. 11:25).

A. SACRAMENT OR ORDINANCE

In general Baptists have asked three questions about religious rites that Christians should observe permanently: Did Jesus command it? Did the Church in the New Testament practice it? Does it have meaning for the believer in the community of believers? As we see it, for example, marriage does not pass the first test, foot-washing fails the second (although a few smaller Baptist bodies do practice it), and the baptism of infants fails all three. In any case we believe that the grace of God is brought into every believer's life by the direct action of the Spirit of God upon the soul and cannot be made effective through an outward act or ceremony.

Historically the battleground has turned at least in part on the word *mere*. Baptists have said, in effect, that grace cannot be conveyed by a "mere" rite, for the Holy Spirit works directly upon the human spirit (I Cor. 2:10–16). Sacramentalists have said, in effect, that the sacraments are more than "mere" symbols, for they also convey the grace they signify.

Now both agree that baptism is a sign and symbol. But signs and symbols point to a reality beyond themselves. They can be means of stimulating or supporting faith, as in the case of Jesus placing clay moistened with spittle on the eyes of the blind (John 9:6). But the healing was not in the clay, nor in the washing in the Pool of Siloam. It was in the power of God operating through human faith. Jesus never limited himself to such material aids or religious observances, such as, "Go show thyself to the priest" (Mark 1:43), for he could on another occasion heal Bartimaeus with nothing more than "Go thy way; thy faith hath made thee whole" (Mark 10:52). In James 5:13–15 the elders of the church are instructed to pray over the sick and anoint him "with oil in the name of the Lord." The anointing with oil was a well-known Old Testament practice that signified the power of the Holy Spirit coming upon someone. So the faith of the sick is stimulated by the anointing and then directed toward the divine power that alone can heal. That this is an experience that touches the sick at the depths of his being is also revealed in that "if he have committed sins, it shall be forgiven him."

To speak of a "mere symbol" as though there were nothing more is to ignore the psychological and social power of symbols. If one were lecturing to a friendly audience of contemporary Jews and suddenly paused and drew upon the chalkboard a swastika, would not that symbol immediately arouse hostility and anguish? The power of symbols lies in the power of the association of ideas, the recalling of emotions, the arousal of the wills. And such power springs from within the psyche, not the symbol or act within itself.

So when Baptists insist upon the ordinances being symbols and not effecting instruments or vehicles of the grace of God they by no means want to play down the importance or the role of the "ordinance." Rather, they want to locate its power and the realm of its operation in the only life-transforming place: the power of the Spirit of God working at the center of one's being. Anything less than this is either ineffectual or can become hypocritical, for we know too many instances when religious rituals have been properly acted out with no shred of evidence that Jesus has been made Lord of the life, and that as well among Baptists also!

Another major Baptist objection to the sacramental system has to do with what is perceived as a flaw in the understanding of *grace*. All will agree that the biblical word primarily refers to the character of God (and of Christ) that causes him to forgive and justify us unworthy sinners (Eph. 2:4–9). Yet when grace is conceived further as a kind of divine effluent that flows from God to man, religious rites—sacraments—are seen as tapping into that flow of grace and channeling it to the sinner. This naturally calls for properly ordained clergy to control the "taps" and instruct the sinner in the right procedure for receiving grace as the end result.

Now Baptists do not accept the latter theory of grace or such power of the clergy. They view that system as violating soul competency. And while acknowledging God's *use* of human agents, they are not willing to trust to the *control* of fallible humans the operating power of the Spirit of God. Present-day Roman Catholic theologians of the sacraments are moving away from such a narrow scholastic and mechanical view of grace. But as long as the sacramental system continues to derive its authenticity from apostolic succession and "valid orders," it will be hard to convince Baptists to withdraw their objections.

Now whether we view these rites as symbols only or as sacraments, all today will agree that it is possible for uncommitted people to go through the motions with no meaning or experiential value whatever. At least the present stage of the debate is making both sides examine more closely our theology and practice in the search for deeper reality in religion.

B. BAPTISM

One of the ironies of history is the widespread misconception that because of our name, Baptists hold that baptism is essential to salvation. It is quite the other way around: the salvation must be experienced (and evidenced, at least in part, by public profession of faith) before baptism has any meaning.

During the Reformation there arose a radical movement

which broke both with the Catholic Church and the Reformers over "believer's baptism." These people who denied infant baptism were called "Anabaptists" (from the word "to baptize again"), because they required a voluntary confession of faith in Christ before baptism. They were called Anabaptists by their enemies, but they did not accept the name. They did not think of "believer's baptism" as a rebaptism, but as true baptism, validated only by their confession of faith. Their direct descendants today are the highly-respected Mennonites.

By the middle of the seventeenth century groups of believers in England and America had carried believer's baptism a further step and had come to insist upon immersion as the only form that carries the full New Testament meaning. Scholars of the Early Church now agree that immersion was the majority practice of the churches of the first three centuries.[1]

Let us look at two Scriptures which influence greatly the Baptist understanding. In Colossians 2:10 through 3:4 Paul is speaking out of his life as a Jew, where his religious privileges were his by right of circumcision. Since he has met Christ, he has rejected inherited religion, with its dependence upon external ceremonies, and obedience to law (Phil. 3:3–9). He has discovered that through faith he has entered into union with Christ. This inward experience has identified him with Christ in the supreme moment of redemption—the death, burial and resurrection of his Lord. By faith he has accepted this act of the love of Christ which has freed him from sin. It is not only an act done by Christ in his behalf at a particular point in history. It is a work done by Christ at the very center of his being. In this he had died, morally and spiritually, to his old self way of living. This is not a drastic asceticism (which he repudiates in vss. 16–23), but a spiritual mystery which brings immediately the opposite effect, that is, an inner resurrection which goes beyond a Lazarus-type restoration to mere human innocence. It is rather the divine life which is Christ himself being born within the believer: "For you have died, and your life is hidden with Christ in God. Your real life is Christ, and when he appears, then you too will appear with him and share his glory!" (Col. 3:3–4, TEV).

Now this kind of mystical baptism into Christ takes place in the realm of the inner life in the act of the believer's commitment of faith to Jesus Christ. The external ceremony depends for its validity upon the reality of the inner experience. This is the reason for believer's baptism.

In the second Scripture Paul is arguing against those who would take advantage of the free gift of God's grace in salvation and so continue in sin. He asks the question, "We who died to sin, how shall we any longer live therein?" (Rom. 6:2). Then he answers his question by stating the fact of the powerful reality behind the act of being baptized and concludes with the practical exhortation: "Even so reckon ye also yourselves to be dead unto sin, but alive unto God in Christ Jesus. Let not sin therefore reign in your mortal body ... but present yourselves unto God, as alive from the dead, and your members as instruments of righteousness unto God" (Rom. 6:11–12). So this "religious rite" is not inconsequential as to its form, for it has strong consequences for one's approach to daily Christian living.

With this instruction, let us look at the meaning of baptism as set forth in the intervening verses.

> Or are we ignorant that all we who were baptized into Christ Jesus were baptized into his death? We were buried therefore with him through baptism into death: that like as Christ was raised from the dead through the glory of the Father, so we also might walk in newness of life. For if we have become united with him in the likeness of his death, we shall be also in the likeness of his resurrection; knowing this, that our old man was crucified with him, that the body of sin might be done away, that so we should no longer be in bondage to sin; for he that hath died is justified from sin. But if we died with Christ, we believe that we shall also live with him (Rom. 6:3–8).

With such a powerful figure of what happens when the believer is united with Christ in the crucial event of death and resurrection, Baptists must make a distinction between this mystical experience wrought by the Spirit and the religious rite of water baptism. George Beasley-Murray makes this clear in commenting on I Peter 3:21, which says, "This water was a figure pointing to baptism, which now saves you, not by washing off bodily dirt, but by the promise made to God from a good conscience. Baptism saves you through the resurrection of Jesus Christ" (TEV). He says, "In so writing the author puts out of court any interpretation of baptism in terms of a purely outward and physical purification or an automatic effect on the baptized. The water of baptism saves nobody. The baptism that saves is one in which the baptized declares his response to God's approach to him in the Gospel, confesses Jesus as Lord, and owns obedience to Him. Baptism is a spiritual act, and this is why the author is so anxious to correct any possible misapprehension of it."[2]

The religious rite of immersion in water then is a symbol of the spiritual act which has taken place in the soul of the one who has in faith responded to the Good News in Christ. To ask for baptism is to carry such faith through to its glad witness to what one experiences in being united to Christ. It is a public testimony, a dramatization of his faith in at least three aspects:

1. He acts out his reliance upon Christ, who died, was buried, and was raised from the dead for his salvation.

2. He acts out his witness to his own spiritual experience of death to the old sinful life and resurrection to a new kind of life as a disciple to a new Master.

3. He acts out his confidence that at the general resurrection of all men he will stand justified before God by reason of his faith in Christ. Now this confidence is more than a subjective hope. It is based upon the believer's present possession of the resurrected life, which is the source of victory in the face of death and the power for the ultimate resurrection from the dead (I Cor. 15:20–22; Rom. 8:11).

Now someone may object—do you mean to say that everyone who is baptized understands all these theological niceties? Hardly. Certainly not to the extent that they can verbalize them as we have done here. Even Saul of Tarsus (Paul) after his Damascus road experience and after his baptism (Acts 9:1–9) needed a season of retreat into Arabia in order to work out his understandings of this life-changing experience (Gal. 1:17).

We have already said that the ability to grasp the meaning of the experience depends upon the extent of the preaching and teaching of the Word and upon the personality and maturity of the believer. Faith is not measured by its content, but by the extent of its commitment. For the most part pastors and churches take seriously their responsibility of preparing the new convert for baptism. Of course, this is most critical with children. In Baptist life there is a continuing debate over the best time for a child to "make his public profession" and ask for baptism and over the best methods of counseling children for baptism. But let it not be thought all that difficult to bring Paul's explanations to bear upon the new convert. The realities of birth and death are basic to all human experience. They are both simple facts that can readily be accepted even by children and profound mysteries that continue to challenge the wisest of adults.

If then the new convert is wisely and patiently counseled and the rite of baptism reverently carried out, the act itself becomes a peak spiritual experience for the one being baptized and for the congregation which has accepted responsibility for his Christian nurture as a new member of the People of God. Baptism, therefore, is authorized by the church and performed publicly before the congregation. It is never a private or family ceremony. "The practical liturgical consequence [of this reinforcement of the church's faith] is clear: in principle baptism cannot be celebrated as a private act or a family festival. In principle it can only be celebrated within the framework of the public worship of God."[3] The present trend in Catholic practice today is to make this rite an integral part of the worship services and not one added thereto.

Baptism is a sign both of the beginning of life in Christ and the acceptance in community by the congregation (a traditional practice, somewhat lax today, is to have all candidates who have been baptized to "receive the hand of church fellowship" at the close of the worship service). Because it is not considered essential to salvation, there is not the urgent necessity to make it a once-for-all event as in the case of the sacramental practice. There are those who, having been baptized as children, come later to experience Christ in salvation for the first time, perhaps years later. They see their former baptismal rite as invalid because it was not based on a genuine experience of salvation. So they ask the church for "valid baptism" based on the reality of the now-genuine experience of salvation.

Because of this meaning of baptism, most Baptist churches will expect those who join them from those that baptize infants or those who have been baptized after confession of faith but not by immersion to ask for "believer's baptism by immersion." This in no way is judging their experience of salvation to be invalid, but is the new member's renewed testimony to his faith in the death, burial and resurrection event. This, by inference as all Christian bodies practice, is the new member's honest acceptance of the beliefs and responsibilities of the body of Christians with whom he is uniting.

The act of baptism today is carried out in the baptismal pool, usually located behind the pulpit and choir loft of the church. The old-timers used to pride themselves on being baptized outdoors and particularly in running water. There was much singing on the river banks, an opportunity for the convert to "make a good confession" of his faith and even such rejoicing as to call forth shouts of praise from both the baptized and his new "brothers and sisters in the Lord."

The pastor and baptismal candidates are robed in white. After being led into the water the pastor proclaims in these or similar words, "In obedience to the command of our Lord and Savior Jesus Christ, and upon your free and public acceptance of him as your Savior and Lord, I baptize you, N_____ N_____, in the name of the Father and the Son and the Holy Spirit. Amen." He then lays the person backward gently into the water, pauses to cover the mouth and nostrils, lowers him just under the surface of the water and immediately raises him upright. As he leads him out of the pool, he may quote a Scripture, such as, "We are buried with him by baptism into death that as Christ was raised up from the dead by the glory of the Father, even so we also should walk in newness of life" (Rom. 6:4, King James Version).

After baptism our churches today often place the convert in a pastor's class or new members' class where he is given special instruction in the resources of the church for his continued spiritual growth as a Christian. After baptism the new convert is now expected also to participate at the regular observances of the Lord's Supper.

Our Baptist theology and practice of "making Christians" is far from perfect. Josef Nordenhaug acknowledges that our critics would argue, "Since there is a widening gap between the principle we profess and the practice of it, should we perhaps set aside the principle of a regenerate church membership in the interest of bringing so many as possible to baptism and under the influence of the church in the hope that their attendance at church services and participation in the educational program of the church may in time produce Christian faith and a life in harmony with it?"[4] But he rejects this argument, which has frequently been used to justify infant baptism. Instead he calls for continuing renewal based upon five points: (1) continual examination of the motives to which we appeal in the churches, especially the success syndrome measured by additions, budgets, and buildings; (2) ridding ourselves of "the weed of self-righteousness that grows so profusely among us. . . . We must cease giving doctrinal reasons for personal grudges"; (3) care not to use worldly, even devilish, means for the propagation and defense of the Gospel; (4) a recovery of the practice of church discipline; and (5) greater use of confessing of sin to one another and of the role of pastoral counseling.[5]

Finally the goal of all religious practices, ordinances, ceremonies should be that called for by the Apostle Paul: "And so we shall all come together to that oneness in our faith and in our knowledge of the Son of God; we shall become mature men, reaching to the very height of Christ's full stature. Then we shall no longer be children, carried by the waves, and blown about by every shifting wind of the teaching of deceitful men, who lead others to error by the tricks they invent. Instead, by speaking the truth in a spirit of love, we must grow up in every way to Christ, who is the head" (Eph. 4:13–15, TEV).

C. THE LORD'S SUPPER

Nothing so proves the perversity of sinful human nature as its penchant for debasing what is pure and profaning what is holy. So it has been in Christian history with the one great religious act which Jesus left to his disciples with the obvious intent of unifying them around the supreme sacrifice of his love, the Cross. In the Eucharist[6] or the Lord's Supper (1 Cor. 11:20) worship rises to its holiest moment. Yet nothing has produced more divisions among Christians than the beliefs and practices of this great act of worship.

63

Let us start with a series of observations upon which most biblical scholars would agree:

1. It was instituted by Jesus on the night before his crucifixion (I Cor. 11:23).

2. It was given in perpetuity to his disciples (I Cor. 11:20, 26).

3. It was to be a "remembering" of Christ (I Cor. 11:24-25).

4. It somehow was a communion of the believers with the sacrificial death (the body and blood) of Christ (I Cor. 10:16-21).

5. This involves the believers in a oneness in Christ (I Cor. 10:17).

6. There was a celebration of the New Covenant which Christ inaugurated by means of his death (Mark 14:24; I Cor. 11:25; cf. Heb. 8:7-13).

7. It looks forward to the final coming of Christ (I Cor. 11:26) and to the Messianic Banquet of the age to come ("until the Kingdom of God is come," Luke 22:18: cf. Matt. 26:29).

8. The presence of Christ is experienced in the event, if for no other reason than Christ's promise, "where two or three are gathered together in my name, there am I in the midst of them" (Matt. 18:20).

Now it would seem that with so many points of agreement Christians would have little to divide over, but not so. Here are just a few issues:

1. Is this a sacrament that conveys the grace of God or an ordinance that commemorates the central fact of the Gospel?

2. Who is admitted to the Supper? Most all agree only baptized persons. But baptized by whom, how and for what purpose? Are there moral and spiritual qualifications? Who judges these?

3. Who administers the Supper, those ordained or simply leaders of the congregation? What constitutes ordination, if this is a prerequisite?

4. Where is the presence of Christ in the event? In the elements? In the worshipers? In the body as a whole?

5. How often should the Supper be observed?

Historically Baptists have involved themselves in these issues and a few of their own making. It is readily agreed that much of our practice grew out of the Reformation reaction to Catholic dogma and to practices which the Reformers deemed magical and abusive. Four hundred and fifty years later these issues are so deeply imbedded in the corporate life of both Protestants and Catholics that no redefinitions of theologians can soon resolve them. This author can only hope to reflect the general views of Baptists here, while recognizing that he will be disputed by other Baptists on many points.

Let us use the five problem issues as a frame to present this Baptist's view of the Lord's Supper.

1. We have dealt with the first problem already under the two previous sections. We will make a few further observations. The Latin word *sacramentum* in secular society meant "a military oath of allegiance." Later tradition took the word and imposed upon it the meaning, "an outward sign of an inward grace." It was not at first applied to any of the seven sacraments.[7] The Council of Trent formally defined the number and the meaning of the seven sacraments in reply to the Reformers (Trent: 1545–63).

With that meaning Baptists begin to get anxious. They can accept the idea of a sign or symbol (even some early and a few present-day Baptists, mostly in England, have used the word "sacrament"). They recognize the power these can have in evoking or recalling profound meanings and feelings. Such signs as words, pictures, music, bodily movements, sculpture, architecture and drama all carry symbolic power. The two disciples on the way to Emmaus recognized Jesus only in his act of breaking bread and giving thanks.

Now Jesus frequently used symbolism to reveal his nature and function to his disciples. He said, "I am the door," "I am the true vine," "I am the way." No one, not even the most literalistic among us, would try to make these other than what was intended, the striking metaphors which they are. Symbols suggest mental and spiritual realities which cannot be contained in literal terms. They are like windows which open upon great vistas. But when symbols become things in themselves and not signs to greater realities, they short-circuit the power of truth. When Jesus spoke to the crowd after the miracle of feeding the five thousand, he said, "Anyone who does eat my flesh and drink my blood has eternal life" (John 6:54, Jerusalem Bible). The Jews were greatly offended because they did take him literally. Drinking of any kind of blood was a major taboo in their Law (Lev. 3:17; Acts 15:20).

So Baptists view the Supper as powerful symbols. The broken bread and the crushed "fruit of the vine" (Luke 22:18) recollect the experience of Jesus in providing our salvation. This evokes our thanksgiving for our own experience of being crucified with Christ so as to come alive in him (Gal. 2:20). It calls forth the sacrifice of our whole selves in response to the sacrifice of Christ which is remembered, and even in a figure reenacted, but not "re-presented" (Rom. 12:1–2). The sharing of the bread and wine calls us to recognize our unity in Christ (I Cor. 10:16–21) and our dependence upon the indwelling Christ for the sustenance of our lives (John 6:54).

Baptists, therefore, react negatively to any use of the symbols which makes them ends in themselves, such as adoration of the elements or the celebration of festivals in their honor. We know our own nature well enough to know we can perform all kinds of religious rites and practices and be devoid of any meaning or reality in the act. So we hold that faith and inner experience alone can give reality to symbolic acts. We also deny the implication that since we do not locate the presence of Christ in the elements, we do not know how to celebrate the real presence in either our individual or our corporate lives and actions. We know our daily lives to be sustained on such divine "flesh and blood" as well as other Christians.

Jesus said, "This do in remembrance of me." In the context of the observance of the Passover, he is asking us for more than just a recalling of the event of the Cross or meditation upon his incarnate life. In the Jewish family's observance of the Passover meal in the home the father and the son engage in the traditional conversation after the drinking of the second cup. The son begins the dialogue by asking, "Why does this night differ from all other nights?" And the father "re-collects" the great event of the Exodus, by which the nation was constituted. Rabbi Solomon Bernards describes the moment during the Passover meal in a Jewish home when the father explains why this night "is different from all other nights." Among other things, "In each generation, every man is duty-bound to envision himself as though he personally took part in the Exodus from Egypt; as we read in the

Torah: 'you shall tell your son on that day, saying, "It is because of what the Eternal did for *me* when I came forth from Egypt." ' It was not only our forefather that the Holy One, blessed be He, redeemed; He redeemed us, the living, together with them."[8] As all the family raise their winecups together they recite: "We should therefore sing praises and give thanks and pour out infinite adoration to Him Who performed all these wonders for our fathers and for us. He brought us from slavery to freedom, from anguish to joy, from mourning to festivity, from darkness to light, and from bondage to redemption; and we will sing unto Him a new song, Hallelujah."[9]

Is Jesus, then, not asking us to relive our union with him in the sufferings of his Crucifixion? Paul spoke of this union both as a past event and a continuing experience: "I have been crucified with Christ; and it is no longer I that live, but Christ liveth in me" (Gal. 2:20). He glories only in the Cross, "through which the world hath been crucified unto me, and I unto the world" (Gal. 6:14).

Now this evoking of the crucial event of our redemption should provoke in us even greater feelings and resolves than those of the Jewish family (for we enter also into the Passover event). Here, unfortunately, the debates over Eucharist versus Lord's Supper are most regrettable, for they obscure the Lord's challenge at the core of our union with him and our participation in the Body of Christ, the Church. For the Supper invites us again and again to enter into the pain and grief of our sin, which fell upon our Brother, as well as the release and joy which he now so graciously gives us. Our overreactions against each other tend to cancel both of us out. Sacramentalists, caught up in the debate, are too concerned to prove that something happens in the words of institution. Non-sacramentalists, likewise, are too concerned to prove that nothing happens. Neither seems very concerned with the moral, spiritual and social consequences of the worshipers' participation in the rite. To parallel only that which Bernards observes above: where is the evidence that we are released into ever wider freedom, renewed joy, a true "festivity," deliverance from self in our subjection to the values and pursuits of an alien society?

Jesus also said, "This cup is the new covenant in my blood"

(Luke 22:20; I Cor. 11:15). As the first covenant constituted Israel as the people of God under the laws and rituals of Moses, so the new covenant creates a new people of God, which rises above all human distinctions of race and status, even those of male and female (Gal. 3:28). We are thereby made one new humanity in Christ (see also Eph. 2:15). It is hard in this light for any Christian body to persist in the hangovers of nationalism, racism and sexism.

The drinking of the cup, which symbolizes the blood of Christ by which we are brought into this new relationship with God, calls forth a renewed dedication to the covenant community: its support, mutual service, and inner discipline. Paul urges support of the weaker brother, even when it involves limiting one's own freedom of conscience (I Cor. 10:23–33). He binds us to serve one another, even when it is burdensome (Gal. 6:2). He warns against abuse of the Supper by the neglect of inner discipline (I Cor. 5) and by uncontrolled individualism (I Cor. 11:20–21). He has also a severe warning of the consequences of neglecting the necessary preparation of self-examination for participating in the Supper (I Cor. 11:27-34). Dale Moody, writing to Baptists, has said, "Controversy over close communion usually centers on the validity of baptism, which all agree precedes the Lord's Supper, but the question of confession of sin and congregational discipline too often drops into the background. It takes far more than membership in a local church holding correct doctrine to qualify for participation in the Lord's Supper."[10]

2. Who should partake of the Supper? Baptists generally have held only those who have been baptized as professed believers in Christ by immersion. There is, however, much latitude in Baptist practice in differing countries and regions upon this generally held belief. On one end there is the strict Landmark view (see below, Part III) that the Supper is restricted to members of the local church only. More in the center is the view that the Supper is open to all "of like faith and order" (namely, other Baptists). On the other end there are those who will accept anyone who knows himself to be a believer in Christ. Most today would not require any further moral or spiritual qualification than that "a man examine himself, and so let him eat of the bread and drink of the cup" (I Cor. 11:28).

Believing that this ordinance was given to the church as a whole, we practice its observance as a corporate act of the body (an ordained minister never felt obligated to celebrate the Supper privately). We do not usually take the bread and wine to those absent from service, largely because such was feared as encouraging a sacramental view of the Supper. Of course, to be consistent we ought to encourage prayerful participation through some kind of visitation to those who are hindered by reason of health or business, and the church in its ministries should help them to feel the outflow of love from the Lord's Table into their own need.

3. Who administers the Lord's Supper? With the understanding of the church and its officers as described in the preceding chapter, it will be evident that the congregation is the administrator of the Supper. When a pastor is called it is usually taken for granted that he is thereby authorized to lead in the observance of the ordinances. But in his absence the church may elect any member, deacon or other. Any member, but usually the pastor or a deacon, may lead in the prayers. These are understood as prayers of thanksgiving and dedication of lives rather than of the "institution" that brings about a change in the elements.

For generations most Baptists have used unleavened bread (as a link with the Passover meal) and unfermented grape juice (as consistent with the usual Church Covenant's position of total abstinence). In some areas Baptists are occasionally using one large loaf of homemade bread and one cup in a more informal setting to stress the unity and participation in the one body (I Cor. 10:16–17). And the practice is growing of making the Lord's Supper the central act of the service rather than an addition to the regular order of worship. In such case the music and the pastor's homily will lead directly into the Supper.

The "Lord's Table" is usually placed in front of the pulpit on the same level with the congregation. The pastor and his assistant, usually the chairman of the deacons, will sit on either side of the table and the deacons on the front pews. After the prayer of thanksgiving for the bread, the pastor breaks a portion of the bread and distributes plates of bread to the deacons, who in turn serve the congregation. All hold the bread until the deacons return and are served by the pastor and he in turn by a deacon. Then the pastor will speak after this manner, "This is my body, which is for you. All of you, eat of it."

Then follows the prayer of thanksgiving for the cup. The same procedure will be followed in serving everyone with small individual cups. These are held until the pastor says, "This is the new covenant in my blood. Drink of it, all of you," and all likewise drink at the same time. In keeping with the history of the night meeting of Jesus and his disciples where they "sang a hymn and went out" (Matt. 26:30), a hymn usually concludes the service.

4. From this discussion it should be apparent that Baptists do not localize the "real presence" of Christ in the elements, but rather in the total event and in the lives of the believers who are present. I Corinthians 3:16 takes into account the Presence in the church as a whole: "Know ye not that ye are temple of God, and that the Spirit of God dwelleth in you?" I Corinthians 6:19 also places the Presence in each individual: "Or know ye not that your body is a temple of the Holy Spirit which is in you, which ye have from God? and ye are not your own; for ye were bought with a price; glorify God therefore in your body." And Jesus promised, "where two or three are gathered together in my name, there am I in the midst of them" (Matt. 18:20).

With such permanent realities of the presence of Christ Baptists see no need for localizing such in the material symbols of bread and wine. This is why many of us do not feel excluded from genuine worship by those communions which do not admit us to the Lord's Table, even though we may keenly feel the barrier to Christian fellowship. On any interpretation the great drama of Christ's atonement is being acted out for our remembrance and we can "return thanks" and say the "Amen."

5. It is freely admitted that the practice of observing the Supper infrequently arose out of reaction to the high-church practice of observing it every Sunday. Baptists understand the frequency from the words "as often as you eat this bread, and drink the cup, ye proclaim the Lord's death till he come" I Cor. 11:26). Since the rite is not held essential to the daily or weekly sustenance of the Christian life, we prefer to observe less often in order (hopefully) to avoid the boredom and triteness that con-

tinually threatens all of our repeated religious acts. One good result of increasing dialogue with other Christian communions today is the growing concern of many Baptists to make our observance more significant in meaning and more powerful in worship than formerly.

D. THE WORSHIP SERVICE

A Catholic priest told of hearing a Baptist pastor speaking on evangelization. The Baptist told how during a Sunday morning worship service he had brought the meeting to a close half an hour early so that he could send all the congregation out to visit prospects for the church there and then. The priest, properly horrified, asked, "Did you do that before or after the Eucharist?" And then it was the Baptist's turn to be horrified!

Of course, this is an extreme case, but it points up the relative disparity in locating the center of worship between Catholics and Baptists. For the one the focus is upon a re-presentation of the Presence for the benefit of the communicants. For the other it is upon challenge-and-response to the Gospel for the benefit of the "unsaved."

Now, of course, evangelism is not the full end of worship. But the proclamation of the Gospel in order to secure response, both of the saved and the unsaved, is central. It is seen in the placing of the pulpit at the center before the congregation (a few churches have what is called a "divided chancel" with pulpit and lectern on either side, and sometimes a divided choir loft, but this has been resisted often as being too "high church"). This is in keeping with the primary emphasis upon preaching, even to the extent that the other portions of the service were looked upon as "preliminaries." It is seen finally in that almost every Sunday service will conclude with an "invitation" (the old-timers called it the altar call), during which not only non-members are invited to "make decisions" but also members come for "rededication" or to announce themselves for special religious vocation.

Let us look at a "typical" order of Baptist worship, recognizing that there will be much more variety displayed than in any of the denominations that have standard orders for worship. The common features are the preaching of the Word, the singing of hymns and gospel songs, prayers, special music, the offering and the invitation. Here is one such order of worship, found most commonly in a middle-class, mostly white congregation:

Prelude

The Call to Worship. Either a scriptural call by the pastor or one sung by the choir.

A Hymn of Praise. By the choir and congregation.

Recognition of Visitors and Announcements. This often now is moved before the Call to Worship so as not to break the rhythm of the worship.

The Reading of Scripture. Either by the pastor, or responsively by the pastor and congregation alternating.

The Pastoral Prayer. The minister seeks to draw together all of the common elements of thanksgiving and supplication on the part of the congregation.

A Hymn of Dedication. Or a Gospel song of witness or challenge.

The Offering. The bringing of tithes and offerings of the people.

Special Music. Either by the choir as an anthem, hopefully in keeping with the theme of the sermon to follow, or by some vocal group.

The Sermon. Chosen by the minister in the light of his prayerful consideration of the needs of the congregation at the moment, although there will be some common themes on special occasions of denominational emphasis. Generally speaking, the only days observed from the liturgical year will be Easter and Christmas. National observances of Thanksgiving, Mother's and Father's Days, Independence Day and Memorial Day receive their due.

The Invitation. Always with a background of an evangelistic or dedicatory gospel song.

Presentation to the Congregation of those making decisions.

The Benediction. A brief prayer by the pastor and sometimes followed by an Alleluia by the choir.

In spite of the fact that Baptists have been comparatively weak in developing a worship service in which the music is well integrated with the theme of the sermon, music plays a very great part in the life of the people. Congregations usually enter heartily into the singing of hymns and gospel songs, often displaying good harmonies even beyond the choir. Churches with no more than two or three hundred members will have a minister of music who is full-time and has staff status. He will often organize "graded choirs" with lay assistants leading choirs for every age group. The youth and adult (or sanctuary) choirs are frequently well trained and can be capable of quite advanced music. Youth choirs also take mission tours in which they use their music and other leadership talents in Vacation Bible schools to help churches in areas where the Baptist churches may just be entering. Handbell choirs for different age groups and even orchestral groups are beginning to be popular. These varied choir organizations in the churches of the Southern Baptist Convention now number over one million, second only to the Sunday School in size of their enlistment.

Baptists have come a long way from our roots, which we trace back to the synagogue, with its reading of Scriptures, prayers and brief comments. Any medium sized Baptist church may strike the outsider as a beehive of activity. Indeed, we are children of American frontiersmen. We are first and foremost activists in religion. However, together with others today, many of us are seeking anew the dimension of spiritual devotion and inner discipline. Worship always is in need of examination and renewal so as to secure the goal:

> But if all speak God's message, when some unbeliever or ordinary person comes in he will be convinced of his sin by what he hears. He will be judged by all he hears, his secret thoughts will be brought into the open, and he will bow down and worship God, confessing, "Truly God is here with you!" (I Cor. 14:24–25, TEV).

NOTES

1. Karl Rahner, et al., eds, "Baptism," *Sacramentum Mundi,* Vol. 1 (New York: Herder & Herder, 1968), p. 138.

2. G. R. Beasley-Murray, *Baptism Today and Tomorrow* (New York: Macmillan, 1966), pp. 36–37.

3. Karl Barth, *The Teaching of the Church Regarding Baptism* (London: SCM Press, 1948), p. 32.

4. Nordenhaug, *op. cit.,* p. 134.

5. *Ibid.,* pp. 146–147.

6. The word is derived from the Greek verb used of Jesus' act of giving thanks before the breaking of bread and the cup: Luke 22:17, 19; I Cor. 11:24. The noun is not used for the Supper in the Greek New Testament.

7. Karl Rahner, "Sacraments," *Sacramentum Mundi,* Vol. 5 (New York: Herder & Herder, 1968), p. 381.

8. Rabbi Solomon S. Bernards, *The Living Heritage of Passover* (New York: Anti-Defamation League of B'nai B'rith, n.d.), pp. 33–34.

9. *Ibid.*

10. Duke K. McCall, ed., "The New Testatment Significance of the Lord's Supper," *What Is the Church?* (Nashville: Broadman Press, 1958), p. 87.

THE PEOPLE
CALLED BAPTISTS

chapter six

WE ARE SHAPED
BY OUR HISTORY

Baptists have continually amazed others, especially their friends in Christian denominations which have a hierarchical or connectional structure. On the one hand our principle of local church autonomy makes it possible for more than two dozen Baptist bodies to exist side-by-side in the United States alone. On the other hand, these autonomous churches can affiliate in such a way as to produce the largest corps of missionaries of any Protestant denomination. They have a strong tendency to be anti-intellectual, yet they have spawned more colleges and larger seminaries than most. There is no Baptist body that can exercise jurisdiction over any church or any other Baptist body, yet they are probably more unified in their doctrine and polity than those denominations which frame church laws. With the widest possible range of education in their ministers and greatest freedom of individual interpretation of the Scriptures, Southern Baptists are generally conservative in doctrine. Even their so-called "liberals" would seem no more than middle-of-the-road when compared with some liberal Protestants.

There is wide diversity in worship styles, continuing debate over the gospel and social strategies, and ever-recurring efforts on the part of some to impose a kind of creedal orthodoxy. But Baptists have learned to live with such diversity because they have come to unite, not around a creed or code, but on the basis of a common commission of the Lord: "Go ye . . . make disciples . . . teaching them . . . all things" (Matt. 28:19–20).

The secret then of Baptist progress is the common loyalty to a divinely given action program. When the Southern Baptist

Convention was formed in 1845 the preamble to the constitution it adopted stated its purpose of "organizing a plan for eliciting, combining and directing the energies of the whole denomination in one sacred effort, for the propagation of the Gospel. . . ." This was later further defined as consisting of "missions, education, and benevolence." Thus, with no authority to intervene in the internal affairs of local churches or other Baptist bodies, the Convention has been free to devote its growing energies to cooperative endeavors that center upon proclamation of the Gospel and ministry to human needs.

How did these "peculiar people" come to be (a term Baptists like to use of themselves with a bit of tongue in cheek, drawn from I Peter 2:9, King James Version)? How have they learned to work together? Why are they so insistent upon "separation of Church and State"? Finally, are they becoming more socially aware and involved? These will be the subjects of Part III.

To render an adequate account of Baptist history is beyond the scope of this book and the capabilities of its author. I can only hope to sketch briefly our origins, the main lines of development and the movements that continue to influence Baptist life. The latter is essential to understanding many of the attitudes today of Baptists toward other Christian groups. Again, because our focus is upon the heritage of Southern Baptists, apologies are needed for the omission of those vital movements that produced the more than twelve million Baptists in other conventions and associations in America. (The interested reader is referred to the bibliography herein.)

A. THE EARLY BEGINNINGS

Caught up in the debate over the "one, true Church," some early Baptist historians sought to prove that Baptists have had continuous existence through many different dissenting groups all the way back to New Testament times. Some of these groups held to the principle of the Scriptures as their only authority. Others held to baptism (but not necessarily by immersion) for believers only. Others held to a radical separation from State and society One of the few things they held in common was dissent from the established church and the consequent persecutions by both

Catholic authorities and Reformers. With the maturing of historical research today, few Baptist historians would try to establish such linear connectionalism.

There is better claim to spiritual, but not organizational kinship with the Anabaptists of the sixteenth century in Northern Europe. While the early Baptists agreed with the Anabaptists on the authority of the Scriptures and believers' baptism, they did not agree with them on their radical renunciation of political oaths and office-holding. Nor did they join in some of the extreme millennial views that produced such terrible slaughter in the Muenster Rebellion in 1535. Contemporary historical research has well established the fact that such armed rebellions did not represent the main body even of Anabaptists, and certainly not of the later Mennonites.[1]

The Puritan movement within the Anglican Church of the sixteenth century in England produced the Separatists, who desired to break with the established church in order to call out believers from the "corrupt establishment." They no longer hoped for any lasting reform within the Anglican fold and so moved toward a "gathered community" of believers bound together by covenant. One of the Separatists was Francis Johnson who taught in Christ's College at Cambridge in 1586 a young student for the Anglican priesthood named John Smyth. In 1600 Smyth was elected preacher of Lincoln. By 1606 he was in his home village of Gainsborough, where a Separatist church was about to divide. One group at Scrooby Manor became the Pilgrim Church that eventually came to America. There Smyth and Thomas Helwys began to question the practice of infant baptism. They came to the conclusion that only believers should be baptized, so Smyth first baptized himself and then led some forty persons of the congregation to be baptized by affusion. Soon he questioned this self-baptism and together with the majority approached the Waterlander Mennonites for admission.[2]

Thomas Helwys, however, with a small group around 1612 returned to England and established the first Baptist church in that country at Spitalfield, just outside London. Since Smyth died the same year, Helwys' group actually becomes the beginning of continuous Baptist life. For his writings and his preaching Helwys was imprisoned, and he died in 1616. His leadership was assumed by John Murton and soon there were forty-seven

General Baptist churches, Arminian in theology, evangelistic in purpose, and dedicated to religious liberty, even at the price of severe persecution at the hands of Archbishop Laud in the reign of Charles I.[3]

The Particular Baptists, who accepted Calvin's view that Christ's atonement was only for the elect, had a different origin. A Separatist congregation led by Henry Jacob was organized at Southwark, near London, in 1616. Several leaders of this congregation, including Jacob, at various times before 1640 sought freedom from persecution by migrating to America, but they met the same in the new land, this time from the early colonists who themselves fled England for religious freedom.

Torbet describes both of these groups as Baptists: "English Baptists of the seventeenth century were clear on what makes a true church. They regarded the church as a gathered community of redeemed men and women who had covenanted to walk together under the discipline of the Word of God and, with a properly appointed leadership, to proclaim the gospel and observe regularly the ordinances. Believer's baptism became the symbol of their identification with the risen Christ through the experience of individual conversion."[4]

By 1638 those Baptists who insisted on baptism for professed believers only came together under John Spilsbury to form the first Particular Baptist church. In 1640 they became concerned over the proper mode of baptism. Led by Richard Blunt they "became convinced that baptism by sprinkling or pouring, whether administered to believers or adults, or to infants, was not the true form of baptism employed in the time of the apostles, but that true baptism 'ought to be by diping [sic] the Body into the Water, resembling Burial & rising again.' "[5]

Blunt found a small group of Mennonites at Rhynsburg in Holland who practiced immersion. From them he took instructions back to his congregation. There he baptized the "teacher," Mr. Blacklock, and was baptized by him. Together they baptized by immersion "the rest of their friends that were so minded, and many being added to them they increased much."[6]

Baptist churches have long puzzled other Christians by their paradoxes: autonomous congregations and denominational cohesiveness; individual interpretation of Scripture and stability of doctrinal beliefs; independence that spawns new churches and institutions coupled with a sense of interdependence that develops unity of mission effort. From their earliest beginnings they have felt the need for some kind of connectional relations. At first the motivation for fellowship among churches was primarily defensive. They were trying to survive in a society that saw the free church system as a threat to its basic political, economic and ecclesiastical unity. And the rejection of infant baptism implied not only a judgment that all others were not Christian, but also a heresy beyond the control of both State and Church. Truly the world was not yet ready for religious liberty and the pluralism of a free Church in a free State.

So the tiny Baptist churches were driven by inner necessity to form associations for mutual encouragement and guidance and for defining themselves to a hostile world. At annual meetings of "messengers from the churches" there would be inquiries related to matters of doctrine or discipline. In 1644 a group of seven churches at London produced a confession of faith as one of the earliest efforts of several churches to declare their true identity. Its apologetic character is seen by the title page of the 1646 edition: "Published for the vindication of the Truth, and Information of the ignorant; likewise for the taking off of those Aspersions which are frequently both in Pulpit and Print unjustly cast upon them."[7] Within one generation Baptists had grown in numbers and in acceptance sufficiently to seek favor with other Dissenters in England by the London Confession of 1677, produced by messengers from more than one hundred churches in England and Wales. While greatly influenced by the Presbyterian Westminster Confession of 1648, it maintained a strong force in all later Baptist confessions, including those produced in America.

B. THE MOVE TO THE NEW WORLD

Baptists have never felt much need for authoritative connections in establishing new churches. The planting of Baptist churches in the New World is a good example. Many who figured largely in those early American churches became Baptists out of other communions over such issues as forced conformity to an established religion, or doubts over the current attempts to reform or purify the extant churches. Other Baptists from England and

Wales came, not as congregations, but as refugees from the persecutions and burdens of the Old World.

Roger Williams is generally accepted as the Baptist pioneer in the New World. He came as an ordained Anglican priest to Boston in 1631 at the age of twenty-eight. A graduate of Cambridge and a protégé of the influential lawyer, Sir Edward Coke, he seemed a choice prospect to become a prominent teacher and pastor in the Puritan churches. But he soon alienated all of the Massachusetts Bay churches by his radical views.

Hounded out of Boston, Salem and Plymouth in succession, he made his way in the dead of winter with the help of those Indian tribes he had befriended to the head of Narragansett Bay. Together with his small family and four men he founded Providence, buying the land from the Narragansett Indians. The settlement soon attracted other Dissenters, and in 1638 the Colony of Rhode Island was formed. The Compact expressly recognized complete freedom for all, with no religious tests being required for any civil rights.

Williams led the little band to search the Scriptures for the true pattern of the Church. Soon they became convinced that infant baptism was not justified by the New Testament and so chose believer's baptism. One Ezekiel Holliman came forward expressing this new commitment. In the absence of anyone so baptized he then baptized Roger Williams, who in turn baptized Holliman and ten others in March, 1639.

Williams in a few months became dissatisfied with his action and soon pulled out of the congregation. The rest of his life he called himself a "Seeker." While he was hardly a Baptist in name very long, he laid the foundation for the first civil government anywhere in the Western world based on full religious liberty. His mantle as leader of Baptists soon fell to Dr. John Clarke, who also had fled the religious strictures of Massachusetts Bay. Williams assisted Clarke and his band of emigrees to buy land from the Indians and establish the second Baptist church in the new land, perhaps as early as late 1639.

Baptists from England and Wales were also attracted to the colonies of Pennsylvania and New Jersey, where they found more freedom than in New England. It was in Philadelphia in 1707 that the first Baptist association was formed by five churches, one the Welsh Tract Church having been organized in

Wales and moved as a body to nearby Delaware. This association produced the first confession of faith in 1742, an adaptation of the Calvinistic Second London Confession of 1677. By 1767 five other associations were formed in North and South Carolina, Virginia and Rhode Island.

C. THE FIRST CONVENTION ORGANIZED FOR MISSIONS

Mutual encouragement, fellowship and counsel were the original motives of these groups of churches. The annual meeting of the association of churches became a time of exchange of letters from each church read to the assembly describing the progress and problems of the isolated congregations. Often requests for interpretation of doctrines and problems of discipline were sent to the assembly. Out of this grew the practice of assigning to a different preacher a doctrinal sermon and later a missionary sermon. Out of the expressed needs for trained pastors grew the establishing of schools and colleges. Financial support was often raised for missionaries in new fields. But this was sporadic and meager until the coming of Adoniram Judson and Luther Rice.

Before 1814 Baptists in America had shared to some extent in missionary societies, such as the Massachusetts Domestic Missionary Society, formed in 1802 to evangelize the Indians. Anyone who paid as much as a dollar a year could be a member regardless of his denominational affiliation. The annual meetings of such donors as could attend elected trustees, set policies and appointed missionaries. These societies had as their pattern such bodies as the London Missionary Society, which in 1792 sent out as its first missionary to India the great pioneer, William Carey. As a method of missionary cooperation this plan appealed to the highly individualistic Baptists, because it completely avoided any tendency toward a connectionalism which might usurp the authority and independence of local congregations.

Baptists shared in the financial support of the American Board of Commissioners for Foreign Missions, established in 1812 by the Congregationalists, and helped send two of their number to India. Traveling separately and knowing they must encounter William Carey's Baptist views on believer's baptism, Judson and Rice each came to accept those views from their independent study of the Greek New Testament. Soon after arriving in Serampore they requested believer's baptism by Carey and sent their resignations as Congregational missionaries to the American Board. When Judson chose to develop missions in Burma it became necessary for Rice to return to the States to seek support for this mission suddenly thrust upon Baptists. Supported at first by a local society in Boston, Rice was able to stir up interest in the Baptist strongholds of Philadelphia, Charleston and Savannah. A convention was called for by a number of associations to meet in 1814 in Philadelphia. There was formed "The General Missionary Convention of the Baptist Denomination in the United States for Foreign Missions," later to be known as the Triennial Convention.

The constitution of the Triennial Convention provided for representation from local and state missionary societies and from other religious bodies which contributed at least one hundred dollars per year. Again the societal method prevailed over any juridical plan and missions became the sole purpose of the unified effort. The method attracted the support of most of the one hundred and fifteen associations of Baptists. In its second year the Triennial Convention established a home missions society. Its first missionary, John Mason Peck, led in 1832 to the founding of the American Baptist Home Mission Society, which figured a decade later in the formation of the Southern Baptist Convention.

Let us return to the early settlement of Baptists in the South. Since the province of Carolina was granted a charter in 1663 guaranteeing religious liberty, it soon attracted many kinds of dissenters. A group of Baptists under the leadership of William Screven migrated from Kittery, Maine, to near Charleston, South Carolina, probably as early as 1683. By 1693 the group had established the first Baptist church south of Delaware at Charleston. Other groups of Baptists soon arrived from England and from the Welsh Tract near Philadelphia.

The "Great Awakening" began about 1725 and swept through all the colonies through the preaching of such pulpit giants as Jonathan Edwards, George Whitefield and the Wesley brothers, John and Charles. The frontier was a fertile field for the kind of camp-meeting revivalism which carried this new emphasis on experiential conversion. Baptists profited and grew in many areas, particularly in the South. But like other denominations they were divided in judgment on this new emotional experience. Regular Baptists tended to frown upon the uneducated excesses of the movement, while Separate Baptists generally applauded. The latter also grew ever more wary of any form of connectionalism that might endanger the independence of the local congregation. The legacy of the Separates is still strong in the rural areas of the South, long after their name has faded. But Baptists profited overall by the Great Awakening by developing a strong evangelistic zeal and by encouraging associations to send missionaries to establish new churches.

D. SOUTHERN BAPTISTS SEPARATE IN 1845

By the mid-nineteenth century Baptists in America were feeling the strong tensions which were soon to plunge the North and South into bitter war. Even apart from the slavery issue cultural polarities and diverse religious strategies probably would have caused the split among Baptists. Those in the North were committed to having separate societies for carrying on each kind of educational and missionary endeavor. They considered this plan the best way of protecting the autonomy of the local church. In the South Baptists were beginning to call for a convention-type organization with the formation of the South Carolina Convention in 1821. This type of organization sought to protect the local church by allowing affiliation of churches only through "messengers," who had no authority to bind the local church, while at the same time electing boards of directors who would establish missions and educational and other agencies.

The issue that triggered the formation of the Southern Baptist Convention was two-fold. There was general resentment that the American Board of Home Missions was neglecting the South and Southwest in the appointment of missionaries. Then in 1844 the Foreign Mission Society refused the recommendation of Alabama Baptists for the appointment of a slaveholder as a missionary. About the same time Georgia Baptists failed in their effort to get the American Board of Home Missions to appoint a slaveholder to a Georgia mission. These decisions by the national societies were contrary to the previous practice of using slaveholders, even as board members. At the previous Triennial Convention meeting a resolution had been adopted which held that cooperation in the work of foreign missions would sanction neither slavery nor anti-slavery. The Southerners felt that the former practice and the present agreement had been violated without Convention consent.

Virginia Baptists then called for a meeting in Augusta, Georgia, in May, 1845, for the purpose of conferring "on the best means of promoting the foreign mission cause, and other interests of the Baptist denomination in the South."[8] The preamble to the constitution adopted by the meeting stated its overall purpose as "eliciting, combining and directing the energies of the whole denomination in one sacred effort, for the propagation of the Gospel."[9] At that meeting both a Foreign Mission Board and a Board of Domestic Missions were organized. Various efforts at establishing a publishing house met with only sporadic success until 1891, when the present Sunday School Board was established. By providing one body of literature for Bible schools and Christian training for the vast majority of Southern Baptist churches, this Board has been one of the strongest unifying forces of the Convention.

Theological education, which had begun as early as 1855 as a department of Furman University in South Carolina (founded in 1829), began in 1859 as Southern Baptist Theological Seminary. Disrupted by the War years it was moved to Louisville, Kentucky, in 1877. Since then five other seminaries have been founded which provided not only theological education, but also education for music ministers, religious educational directors, social workers, missionaries, and a growing list of specialists. The Convention funds their tuition and fees are kept low so that married students, who are in the majority, may be able to get a theological education, usually while working part-time or serving as student pastors. In 1977–78 the six seminaries reported over eleven thousand students in all schools.

E. OTHER DIVIDINGS LEAVE THEIR MARK

The nineteenth century which witnessed the beginnings of a national organization brought also an era of divisions. There had been some losses to Unitarian and Universalist movements in New England in the latter part of the eighteenth century, but these had little appeal to the growing churches on the frontier. The latter, though, were peculiarly susceptible to various anti-mission movements. Naturally suspicious of any centralized authority, they also opposed an educated and salaried clergy, Sunday Schools, Bible unions, missionary societies and, among the hyper-Calvinists, evangelistic efforts. Alexander Campbell, who was of independent Presbyterian background from Ireland, joined briefly with Baptists in 1813. By 1820 his strong preaching of baptismal regeneration (i.e., that water baptism is necessary to the salvation experience) began to alienate his fellow Baptists. Campbell's followers sought to reform the churches and restore the pristine conditions of the apostolic era and by 1844 were calling themselves simply "Disciples." They hoped to unify all Christians around the New Testament alone with the slogan, "Where the New Testament speaks, we speak; where the New Testament is silent, we are silent." On such basis they have (in their conservative wing, the Churches of Christ) renounced musical instruments in worship and also such officers and organizations in the churches as cannot be specifically justified by the New Testament. Decrying all denominations and divisions they produced yet another. Baptists suffered considerable losses to this movement in the states along the Ohio River.

By far the most influential nineteenth-century movement on Southern Baptists was that called "Landmarkism." Beginning in the 1850's through the preaching and writings of J. R. Graves, editor of *The Tennessee Baptist,* Landmarkism held that Baptist churches were the only true Church. The name was taken from a favorite text, "Remove not the ancient landmark, which thy fathers have set" (Prov. 22:28). This was applied to what they considered to be ancient Baptist principles. In the latter half of the century denominational rivalry provided a fertile soil for the rapid spread of Landmark ideas. In brief, these are:

1. Baptist churches began in the New Testament and can be traced through baptismal succession in many of the persecuted sects of the Middle Ages. As such they are not "protestants," for they had never been in the Catholic Church and they were never a part of the protesting groups in the Reformation. (No reputable Baptist historian today holds to this historically impossible theory; yet some "Letters to the Editor" in Baptist papers will occasionally take this position.)

2. Since Baptists are the only true church, ordination in other denominations was not considered valid. Therefore, their administration of baptism and the Lord's Supper was also invalid. Pulpit exchange, which Baptists hitherto had generally practiced, especially with Presbyterians and Methodists, was completely forbidden.

3. The only valid baptism, therefore, was that of a Baptist church. So even immersion on a profession of faith by other than Baptist churches was not recognized. This was called "alien immersion."

4. Since the local congregation is the only valid church, there was no recognition of a church universal. The Lord's Supper was limited to the local members, as being the only ones under proper discipline. This was called "closed" or "close communion." Furthermore, this emphasis on the local congregation made Landmarkers exceedingly wary of any form of connectionalism, even those societies and agencies formed to support missions. Beginning in 1905 many of the Landmark churches pulled away from affiliation with the Southern Baptist Convention and formed their own denominations, chief of which in the Southwest is the Baptist Missionary Association of America.

The Landmark influence is still felt in certain geographical areas, but it has not greatly slowed the growth of cooperation among Southern Baptists in their pursuit of their stated objectives of missions, education and benevolence.

In the mid-nineteenth century Baptists contributed yet another to the large number of millenarian (see Glossary) leaders of that troubled time. William Miller from Low Hampton, New York, in 1833 began prophesying the return of the Lord for 1843. When he changed the date to 1844 and nothing happened, many of his followers fell away. These "adventists" formed their own denomination which attracted many Baptists.

At about the same time J. N. Darby, a priest of the Anglican Church, who lived mostly in Ireland, left his church over his view that all the established churches were apostate by New Testament standards. He and the Plymouth Brethren, of which he was an influential leader, gave to American evangelical Christianity the first great impetus to "dispensationalism."

Oversimplifying and abbreviating, we may describe dispensationalism as a way of interpreting Scriptures by dividing it into seven historical "dispensations"—the age of innocence to the Fall of Man, from Adam to Noah, Noah to Abraham, Abraham to Moses, Moses to Christ (the Age of Law), Pentecost to the Second Coming of Christ (the Church Age), and the Millennium.

This ingenuous method of interpreting Scriptures seems innocuous enough, but it has had great influence among Baptists and others in forming a popular theology of far reaching consequences. Dispensationalism found its major vehicle of influence in the *Scofield Reference Bible*, the King James Version with notes edited in 1909 by C. I. Scofield, then pastor of the First Congregational Church of Dallas, Texas. It has been popularized also by many Bible Institutes and Bible prophecy conferences, and through a continuing volume of tracts and popular works by C. H. Mackintosh *(CHM's Notes)*, D. L. Moody, Clarence Larkin, and most recently Hal Lindsey *(The Late Great Planet Earth:* Zondervan, 1976). While it has never been either approved or renounced by any major Baptist body, it has had wide influence and an acquaintance with its themes is essential to understanding attitudes and issues among Baptists.

Again oversimplifying, we observe these features which the seven-era system has gathered as it developed into a full theological system. Christ came to establish the Kingdom, but the Jews rejected him. The fulfillment of all the Old Testament prophecies concerning the Kingdom and Jesus' ethical teachings about it are in abeyance until the Second Coming. The Church Age, from Pentecost to his secret return to "rapture" the Church (catch up true believers to Heaven), is the "times of the Gentiles." The true Church is in secret composed of all true believers; all organized churches, Protestant and Catholic, make up a rapidly corrupting Christendom (often the Pope is seen as the high-priest serving the anti-Christ). Efforts to reunite all churches is a sure sign of the end of this age. The only hope is to evangelize individuals and save them from the corruption of the institutional church. God is preparing the land of Israel for the return of Christ to establish his worldwide rule from Jerusalem, and through the Jews (who will be converted en masse) the whole world will be evangelized. Bible prophecies which have not already been literally fulfilled will come to pass at the end time. The Bible is to be interpreted literally, except when dispensational criteria suggest allegorical interpretations.

It is easy to see how this system of Bible use develops an almost wholly other-worldly view of salvation and the Christian's worldview. Under this there is no value in social reform, except as it ameliorates the plight of victims. Ecumenism takes on a sinister purpose. Missions have no other end than making converts. The Cross becomes an after-thought of Christ in view of the failure of his original purpose. The Sermon on the Mount is not to be applied to the Church Age, for it belongs rather to the Kingdom Age (the Millennium). The pursuit of missions in the world is ambivalent, for when the Millennium comes the Jews will be the great effective evangelizers where Christians have failed.

F. THE TWENTIETH CENTURY GROWTH

As we move into the twentieth century we are in the period of Southern Baptists' greatest growth and expansion out of the original eighteen southern states (from Maryland through the Old South to New Mexico and north to Missouri, Southern Illinois and the Ohio River). The most significant factor in this growth was the formation of the "Cooperative Program" in 1925. Prior to that time agents from all the mission boards, seminaries, and other causes had sought financial support by direct appeals to the local churches. In the wave of optimism after the First World War, Southern Baptists challenged themselves to raise $75 million in one great effort for the expansion of all their missionary and educational endeavors. More than $98 million was pledged, but a post-war recession kept the actual receipts in the five-year period to $58.5 million. Meanwhile all agencies expanded their work greatly and new institutions were established. By the time of the 1929 stock market crash, all programs were heavily in debt.

The experience, though, taught Southern Baptists improved ways of stewardship and financial planning. In 1925 a unified budget, called the Cooperative Program, was adopted which allocated on a percentage basis all funds collected. The state conventions became the main collection agencies, deciding in their own meetings what proportion of monies received would be retained for state programs and institutions and what would be sent to the Executive Committee of the Southern Baptist Convention. The latter then disbursed the national funds according to a percentage budget adopted each year at the annual meeting of the Convention (in recent years the percentage plan has been changed to dollar amounts). This financial plan has been supplemented by annual offerings at Christmas for Foreign Missions and at Easter for Home Missions, largely promoted by the organizations of the Woman's Missionary Union, an auxiliary of the Convention since 1888, and the Brotherhood Commission, a movement of Baptist men and boys in missionary support and action since 1907.

These two lines of financial support have provided another strong unifying factor, along with the Sunday School Board, for the more than 35,000 churches affiliating with the Southern Baptist Convention. While there are other unifying forces, such as loyalty to the Scriptures, voluntarism in religion, and defense of religious freedom, none is perhaps as powerful as this dedication to missions and evangelism. This emphasis is not necessarily a distinctive, for there are other denominations which show more missionary zeal, such as the Seventh Day Adventists and the Christian and Missionary Alliance, but it does locate the center of unity for Southern Baptists.

NOTES

1. Franklin H. Littell, *The Free Church* (Boston: Beacon Press, 1957); William R. Estep, *The Anabaptist Story* (Grand Rapids: Eerdmans), 1975.

2. Robert G. Torbet, *A History of the Baptists* (Valley Forge: The Judson Press, revised edition, 1963). I am indebted largely to Dr. Torbet's excellent book for much of this early history.

3. *Ibid.*, p. 69.

4. *Ibid.*, p. 55.

5. Quoted from the Kiffin Manuscript, *Ibid.*, p. 42.

6. *Ibid.*, p. 43.

7. Lumpkin, *op. cit.*, p. 153.

8. Robert A. Baker, *A Baptist Source Book* (Nashville: Broadman Press, 1966), p. 113.

9. *Ibid.*, p. 116.

chapter seven

WE COOPERATE RATHER
THAN LEGISLATE AS
A DENOMINATION

There is a quaint account of a meeting of a Baptist congregation in the autobiography of one of the early missionaries of the American Board of Home Missions that reflects much of the way Baptist churches operated in the past. In Jacob Bower's field in Southern Illinois in 1834 the whole area had recently been sown with very strong anti-mission prejudices. Luther Rice and his helpers were struggling mightily against such resistance. Lack of education among the frontier preachers, fear of centralized authority, reports that "missionaries" taxed each person twenty-five cents for every sermon preached, and Calvinistic views that God needed no human means to convert the heathen—all these combined to make many denounce "missionism" as heresy. But let Bower tell the story in his own unique spelling.

On the saturday following, oct. 18th I went to Mt. Giliad church meeting, to the house where they had all along been in the habit of holding her meetings—and to my astonishment, and surprize of the whole congregation too. The good man of the house, publicly forbid me from preaching on that day. But, said I, it is our church meeting day in course, and you voluntarily gave us your house for that purpose, and our rules of decorum requiers the conference to be opened & closed by prayer & praise. You may pray and exhort, said he, but you shall not preach in my house any more. So we opened our meeting as usual—Noticed those offending members who had abruptly broken off in disorder, and formed a new church, and excluded them. (he one of the number) Then exhorted the church to steadfastness in the cause in which she had embarked [as a "missionary" church]. And to carry it tenderly toards our ering brethren, that they with loving kindness mite be won, and be restored again to the bosom of the church. "Hush and sit down, said he, or go out of my house, for you mite as well preach as to be talking in that way." And this was the last time the church met in his house. But the new church he bid welcome [composed of the excluded anti-mission people]. But the church in a short time gained more than she had lost, and there was not a Dog left in the church to bark against the cause of Missions.[1]

There is so much here that shows both the strength and the weakness of Baptist polity. A congregation has to meet for its monthly business in the home of a member. A layman tries to tell the itinerant preacher what he can and cannot preach. The congregation votes to exclude the "offending members" because they had so disturbed the good order of the church that they had formed a new congregation. The preacher's "exhorting"—public urging of the people to some Christian conduct or attitude, usually by the unordained—here "mite as well" be preaching! The rapid growth of the congregation when unity is restored around the Gospel motive of outreach to others, "missionism," is the result of inner discipline. The congregation needs no ecclesial authority beyond itself to determine its members, its discipline, and its policies.

A. THE UNDERLYING PRINCIPLES OF BAPTIST POLITY

Now affairs in contemporary Baptist churches do not often arrive at such critical states, but the basic principles are still operating today. One way of looking at these principles and forces at work is through the following five pairs:

1. Competency of the soul plus regenerate church membership equals congregational polity. James Sullivan distinguishes this kind of democratic polity as "theodemocracy"—the rule of God revealed in the democratic process: "By New Testament

standards, a church should be a theodemocracy. In a democracy each person may be interested in his own rights and privileges. He may be looking after his own welfare. . . . A democracy can be filled with much self-centeredness. A theodemocracy uses democratic processes to find the will of God instead of the will of men. Each member's judgment is guided by prayer, Bible Study, and conscience. Each one votes what he thinks the will of God is concerning the church."[2] Sullivan points up the advantages of this when the congregation operates while consciously relying upon the guidance of Christ's spirit. It inculcates unselfishness in the individual deferring to the will of the majority, while it gives him freedom of expression of mind and feelings. Since some matters require study and work in committees in preparation, it promotes individual growth. It demands maturity on the part of the majority in protecting the right of the minority.

It is, of course, true today that large churches with highly complex programs of education, music, and ministries are following the pattern of a modified democracy. Pastoral leadership often requires a staff of professionally trained ministers. Business affairs are carried out by committees and church officers who have their functions well defined by the church's constitution and by-laws. But all these are ultimately accountable to the congregation in the times of meetings for business.

2. Local church autonomy plus interdependence of churches equals denominational structure. *Authority* in polity for Baptists operates at no other level than the local congregation. Mutual support and means of kingdom business depend upon the practical measures and structures of *interdependence.* Yet each Baptist body is autonomous with respect to every other. The structures for the denomination are not jurisdictions.

3. Voluntarism plus lay leadership equals internal growth. Even in those large churches with multiple staffs most of the work is done by the laity. The success of Baptists in Bible study for all ages and for personal evangelism lies here. With many small units in education, music, mission organizations and support committees, a large corps of lay volunteers is required. Since there are many reasons for periodic turnover of these people, a continuing program of enlisting and training of new lay workers is required. It is hardly to be claimed that in one hour a week in Sunday School much serious Bible study can be accomplished.

But the teachers and those who train them are spending several hours a week in such study. With at least fifty percent of the active members engaged in these programs it does not take many years to develop an intelligent, dedicated laity.

4. Cooperation plus the leadership principle equals aggressive programs of mission, education, and benevolence. With no hierarchy and no juridical structure Baptist denominations are shut up to using the leadership principle. This means that influence of trusted leaders, gifted with the charisms of speech and psychological skill, can either be a bane or a blessing. Baptists can be taken in by leaders whose hidden aims are power and glory. But the checks and balances developed through many years of struggle and controversy have been built into the association and convention structures to avoid this as far as possible.

5. Decentralization of agencies plus trusteeship equals a denomination that serves the local churches in their autonomy while providing lines of accountability. Some denominations have chosen to place all of their work of missions, education and benevolence under an executive board. Many of the state conventions of Southern Baptists are so organized. But the founding fathers of the Convention determined not to follow this pattern, for they "feared such a board at this level because this is the only place in the denomination where a hierarchical structure could evolve."[3]

Instead in 1927 the Convention created an executive *committee* with responsibility for coordinating the work of the Convention between annual sessions. But they retained separate boards of directors for each of the agencies, institutions and commissions of the Conventions. The Committee has been given the responsibility of receiving monies from the states for the "Cooperative Program" and of disbursing them according to the financial plan reviewed at each annual Convention.

B. HOW DOES BAPTIST POLITY WORK?

Let us review these lines of polity and add a few other notes. Each local congregation is autonomous. It adopts its own constitution, by-laws, church covenant and confession of faith. It calls and appoints its own pastors and deacons. It determines its own programs and sets its own style of worship and observance of the ordinances. It decides the manner and extent of its cooperation with the agencies of the denomination and with other Christian bodies. It determines its own financial plan and seeks to develop its members in Christian stewardship. Legally the autonomy is pure. In practice, it can be strongly influenced by leaders, both within the congregation and in the various Baptist bodies. It reflects cultural and racial differences, for on a given Sunday in the United States there will be Baptist services in as many as seventy different languages and dialects. It is not immune to all the stresses of the society in which it lives, including being influenced by the business and political world around it.

The *association* is the first level of cooperation. A number of churches in a given geographical area (in strongly Baptist areas usually a county) send "messengers" to the annual meeting. There reports will be heard on the progress of all the churches, and plans and reports will be discussed about the various missions and support activities sponsored by the association. An executive board may be formed, made up of a pastor and one lay person from each church, to carry on the work of the association between annual meetings. A "director of missions" and possibly other professional staff may be employed to direct the programs of the association. Here also is the prime arena in which the state and Southern Baptist Convention offer programs and services for assisting the churches in training leaders in religious education, missions and social ministries.

The *state convention* is the next level of cooperation. It elects boards of trustees for the direction of colleges, universities, Bible institutes, benevolent homes, hospitals and other institutions. As with the association the churches send messengers to the annual meeting. These are not called delegates, because in the light of the polity described here an autonomous church cannot delegate authority to another Baptist body. Nor does it authorize its messengers to speak for the congregation, and the actions of the convention are not returned by the messengers with binding force upon the congregation. Resolutions which may be adopted at the convention are expressions of the best mind and will of that particular group of Baptists and carry only influential value for the people back home.

The *Southern Baptist Convention* is the national level of cooperation representing churches in all fifty states which are presently affiliated in thirty-three state conventions and 1,191 associations (1978). It supports seven commissions: Brotherhood, Christian Life, Education, Historical, Radio and Television, Stewardship, and the American Baptist Theological Seminary (jointly with the National Baptist Convention, U.S.A.) for black ministers, at Nashville. There are six seminaries: Louisville, Fort Worth, New Orleans, Wake Forest, North Carolina, Golden Gate, California, and Kansas City, Missouri. In 1977 the Foreign Mission Board reported 2,776 missionaries working in ninety countries. These are involved as consultants to national Baptist conventions, as evangelists, seminary teachers, doctors and nurses, agricultural consultants, publishers, musicians and several others.

The Home Mission Board with a mission force of 2,830 (1978) operates fourteen kinds of mission programs in the fifty states, Puerto Rico and American Samoa. Among these programs are evangelism, church planting, church loans, social ministries, language missions, associational services, black church relations, rural and urban ministries, interfaith witness and the different kinds of chaplaincies.

The *Baptist World Alliance* is a fellowship of Baptists from one hundred and fifteen countries of the world representing more than twenty-nine million Baptists. It sponsors a World Congress every five years to promote religious liberty, world relief and Bible distribution. It provides a forum for the exchange of Baptist views and trends from its many diverse affiliating Baptist groups. The North American Baptist Fellowship is a department of the Alliance which provides some interchange among eight separate Baptist bodies. Most of these also cooperate in the support of the Baptist Joint Committee on Public Affairs in Washington, D.C., which serves as an information gathering agency to keep Baptists in the United States informed of congressional actions which may affect the churches and denomination. It is especially concerned about any legislation which might endanger the separation of Church and State.

C. BAPTISTS AND THE ECUMENICAL MOVEMENTS

The checkered history of Baptist relations with other Christian bodies, especially in the ecumenical movements of the pres-

97

ent century, is too complex for adequate treatment here. We can only sketch the main outline.

As far back as 1890, even before other denominations were showing concern for Christian unity, the Southern Baptist Convention, meeting in Fort Worth, Texas, passed a resolution calling for a kind of Faith and Order conference. The resolution read in part:

> Resolved, By the Southern Baptist Convention representing 1,200,000 communicants, that we recognize the gravity of the problem of bringing different denominations to see alike on important subjects concerning which they now differ, and that we recognize in the teaching of Scripture the only basis on which such agreement is either possible or desirable.
>
> Resolved, That we respectfully propose to the general bodies of our brethren of other denominations to select representative scholars, who shall consider and seek to determine just what is the teaching of the Bible on the leading points of doctrine and polity between the denominations, in the hope that they can, at least, help to a better understanding of the issues involved. . . .[4]

Nothing much came of the proposal. Southern Baptists rejected the report of the Edinburgh Missionary Conference of 1910, which is generally accepted as the beginning of the modern ecumenical movement, on the ground that the Conference avoided any recognition of evangelical missions in "papal lands." However, the Foreign Mission Board was active in the Foreign Mission Conference of North America from 1893–1919 and 1938–1950, when the latter was incorporated into the National Council of Churches. The Sunday School Board has had continuous representation on the International Sunday School Lesson Committee. There have been many examples of working representation by local churches and certain associations and conventions on various kinds of *ad hoc* missions and service programs. Local and some state councils, usually those concerned with civic righteousness, have also attracted Baptist participation. Large evangelistic crusades involving a wide spectrum of denominations, such as the Billy Graham Crusades and Key '73, have the enthusiastic cooperation of most Baptists.

The high-water mark of the Convention's interest in Christian unity was expressed in the report of the Committee of Christian Unity to the 1916 meeting. Southern Baptists were encouraged to continue participation in the fledgling movements for three reasons: (1) Baptists need to help others see that real Christian union can only come on the basis of complete separation of Church and State; (2) Baptists can give a witness to a unity of faith and order based on the freedom of Baptist polity rather than on a "vast Ecclesiasticism"; (3) unity as distinguished from uniformity can be seen in the way Baptists embrace "all classes and conditions of men."[5]

The major turning point came with the address of the president of the Convention in 1919. J. B. Gambrell denounced the unionists for getting control of "camp pastors" (non-military preachers from many denominations) who had been allowed freedom to hold services on military bases. Due to the efforts of John R. Mott, the YMCA was granted exclusive control of the Protestant ministers, while continuing freedom was granted to Jewish rabbis and Catholic priests. The War Department had refused the overture of a joint committee of Northern and Southern Baptists to redress their grievances. On the basis of this affront, Gambrell called upon Baptists to withdraw from all unionizing movements lest the freedom of Baptists to preach the Gospel and make converts be subverted.

There were additional efforts at the time to establish "comity agreements" whereby certain territories both at home and on foreign fields would be assigned to a given denomination, all others being excluded. Also Baptists have always shied away from any kind of "super Church" or world-wide hierarchical structure. Finally, the trend of early leaders of the Federal Council of Churches toward the "social Gospel movement" among liberal Christian denominations effectively closed the door to any significant Southern Baptist participation in the ecumenical movement.

There is some evidence of a new spirit of openness among Southern Baptists. Some have seen that other Baptist bodies cooperate in the National Council and World Council of Churches without loss of freedom or distinctiveness (e.g., the three Black Baptist Conventions and the American Baptist Churches). The 1966 Convention expressed what is probably the majority view of Southern Baptists: "While the majority of our people are not ecumenically minded in a structural and organizational sense, nevertheless, we rejoice with others in the present-day signs of a growing spirit of respect and good will among many religious bodies. We believe that it is the will of Christ that all who believe on him should be of one accord in spirit."

While Southern Baptists voted not to send an official observer to the Second Vatican Council, there were some unofficial observers present for several of the sessions. Scholars and laity alike have followed the progress of the Roman Catholic Church in its spirit of change and renewal with considerable interest. For the past ten years there have been continuing dialogues between scholars and denominational leaders, both regionally and state-wide, of Southern Baptists and Roman Catholics. The Department of Interfaith Witness of the Home Mission Board in its effort to develop bridges of understanding with peoples of all world religions has also conducted dialogue events together with leaders of the Greek Orthodox Church in America, the American Lutheran Council, Buddhist leaders in Hawaii, leaders of the Reorganized Church of Latter-Day Saints, Independence, Missouri, and a few of the Islamic leaders in the United States.

Finally, much real cooperation and mutual support between Baptists and other Christian groups take place on the mission fields of many countries of the world. Confronted with the challenges of non-Christian world religions, communistic societies, and growing anti-American nationalisms, missionaries can ill afford the isolationism that often is a given in predominantly Christian countries.

D. HOW ARE DISSENT AND DISCIPLINE HANDLED?

It is necessary to approach this question from the principles of Baptist polity which have been set forth above. For the individual Baptist, dissent and discipline are solely within the body of covenanted members of the autonomous congregation. Past generations, especially those living on the wide-open and often lawless frontiers, took very seriously their responsibility to discipline the moral conduct and the doctrinal views of their members. Historians agree that often this discipline served as the only curb against immorality and even criminal conduct in society. It is interesting to peruse the records of business meetings of some of the Kentucky Baptist churches in the early nineteenth century. The following indicates some of the disciplinary concerns:

Br. Baker Ewing is Excluded from this Church for Intoxication, for misusing his Wife, & disobeying the call of the Church.

Agreeable to Citement Bro. Pullum came before the Church and Acknowledged his fault; the Church agree'd to bear with him.

A motion made & seconded that this Church fall upon some measure respecting Members of this Church who have mov'd out of the bounds of the Church without applying for letters of Dismission.

A Motion was brought in and Debated on the new system of Principles call'd Herrisy & at length the following Question was taken, is the Son of God Equal & Eternal with the Father? It was Answer'd by a great Majority in favour of the Son being equal with the Father, then the Minority was call'd upon to give their reason for Voting as they did. Several of them Answer'd they were not moved from their old faith.

Sister Hicklin & Sister Stephens profess'd to the Church their reconciliation to each other.

A Charge was brought against Bro. Isaac Miles for saying that Bro. John Bohanan did cover the truth with lies of Hypocrisy, and he was Excluded for the same.[6]

The standard of judgment in all these matters was taken from the congregation's understanding of the teachings of the New Testament, the Church Covenant and Confession of Faith adopted by that church, and from its constitution and by-laws. If a member felt that he was being unjustly judged, he could appeal to the church to call for a council of brethren representing other churches nearby. After hearing both sides the council would retired, debate their judgment, and report back to the congregation in session. As often as not the church might reverse its stand in the light of the advice of the council, but in any case their vote was the determining one.

As the twentieth century saw the rapid growth of members in the churches and the beginning of expansion out of the original eighteen states, Southern Baptists began to shift the focus of discipline to preventive education and reliance upon the mores of the Christian group.

Baptists have long been known for their vigorous stand against alcoholic beverages. The more conservative among them were also against popular dancing and card playing. These were all "sins of the flesh" which not only were sins in themselves but led to greater sins. Baptists were leaders in the movement for Prohibition and lobbied actively at every level against the "evils of drink." There is still strong preaching against drinking and for active involvement at state and local levels with those councils which have been organized for total abstinence. But one today rarely hears of a church excluding a member for drunkenness, although action might be taken against one who operates a liquor business.

Dissent takes a somewhat different approach. With the polity Baptists espouse they are obliged to give a fair hearing to any dissenter, whether in the local church or in the convention. Often when the congregation considers his dissent valid such a person showing the spirit of Christ will be able to change the direction of the church's thinking and action. But if he proves recalcitrant and his dissent threatens the peace of the church, he may in extreme cases be excluded. More often than not he will simply withdraw from the fellowship, pull as many followers as he can with him and form a new congregation. This regrettable course can cause much pain and loss, but in the Baptist system this need not affect the whole of the Baptist fellowship of the area and renewal of the church is always a good prospect.

Again the dissent of a church against an association or convention is another matter. Sometimes as in the case of the "withdrawing of fellowship" by associations in Dallas and Cincinnati recently over a few churches who entered "the tongues movement," the association presses charges against the local church. If a church becomes disaffected with the doctrinal or policy stands of the association and/or convention, it may withdraw its affiliation and "go independent," that is, to go it alone without affiliating with any Baptist body.

Dissent in the Southern Baptist Convention is an ever-present reality. Although annual meetings today have reached as many as 20,000 registrants (Atlanta, 1978), the Convention is still operated on the style of a town meeting where any qualified messenger has the right to make a motion or present a resolution. After many tedious experiences over critical matters, great and small, the Convention has adopted a plan to channel issues. Resolutions must be offered in writing and referred to a resolutions committee for study and report to another session of that meeting. Any motion or resolution with regard to the inner working of one of the boards or agencies of the Convention must be submitted without debate to the proper board of directors for study. These must report to the next annual meeting what disposition they made of the matter. Under the trustee system this keeps the Convention in session from trying to run the internal affairs of its agencies from the floor, while at the same time requiring responsible hearing of any issue raised.

C. Burtt Potter, Jr., in his book, *Baptists: The Passionate People,* finds the motivation for much of the debates and sometimes divisions among Baptists in eight "passionate concerns": for the authority of the Bible, personal redemption, the Church, doctrinal principles, God's Spirit, Southern culture, Christian ethics, and for an exemplary witness. His book is an excellent source of understanding of the critical issues that have been a part of the life of Southern Baptists in the twentieth century.[7]

NOTES

1. William Warren Sweet, *Religion on the American Frontier: The Baptists, 1783–1830* (New York: Henry Holt & Co., 1931), p. 218.

2. James L. Sullivan, *Rope of Sand with Strength of Steel* (Nashville: Convention Press, 1974), p. 40.

3. *Ibid.,* p. 50.

4. Raymond O. Ryland, *A Study in Ecumenical Isolation: The Southern Baptist Convention* (unpublished Ph.D. dissertation, Marquette University, 1969), pp. 67–68.

5. *Ibid.*, pp. 104–105.

6. Sweet, *op. cit.*, "The Records of the Forks of Elkhorn Baptist Church, Kentucky, 1800–1820," pp. 293–308.

7. C. Burtt Potter, Jr., *Baptists: The Passionate People* (Nashville: Broadman Press), 1973.

chapter eight

WE ARE CHAMPIONS
OF RELIGIOUS LIBERTY

"Every man must give an account of himself to God, and therefore every man ought to be at liberty to serve God in that way that he can best reconcile it to his conscience."[1] So wrote Baptist pastor John Leland in "The Rights of Conscience" during the important struggle in the 1780's in Virginia to pass a bill of rights that would guarantee religious liberty. The state had long established the Anglican Church.

Leland went on to refute the oft-repeated claim that the highest good of the State is fostered by a single, established Church so as to produce unity and promote good order.

> Government has no more to do with the religious opinions of men than it has with the principles of mathematics. Let every man speak freely without fear—maintain the principles that he believes—worship according to his own faith, either one God, three Gods, no God or twenty Gods; and let government protect him in so doing, i.e., see that he meets with no personal abuse or loss of property for his religious opinions. Instead of discouraging him with proscriptions, fines, confiscation or death; let him be encouraged, as a free man, to bring forth his arguments and maintain his points with all boldness; then if his doctrine is false it will be confuted, and if it is true (though ever so novel) let others credit it. When every man has this liberty what can he wish for more?[2]

There is no nerve in Baptists that is more sensitive than that which activates our conscience for religious liberty. Critics may accuse us of knee-jerk reactionism, of selective application of the principles, or of championing the cause only when Baptists are a despised minority, but with no shaking of our stand. On this we have a kind of race memory that goes back to our forebears, the Anabaptists of northern Europe in the sixteenth century. It is not just a cause that may need to be espoused on those occasions when we are an endangered species. Nor is it one which lies ready to hand whenever we need to prove our concern for justice for oppressed peoples. These may be the only times the public media take note. On the contrary, religious liberty is an essential part of the warp and woof of the whole cloth all Baptists wear. Even when fighting for this liberty for ourselves, we believe that it is a divine right that promotes the highest good of all men and their societies, even those who oppose us.

A. THE BAPTIST VIEW SHAPED BY OUR ORIGINS

1. *The Anabaptist Heritage.* The Swiss Anabaptists in the 1520's took their stand for believer's baptism and a church "gathered" out of both the established Church and the dominant State. For this the Church accused them of heresy and the State of sedition. The first Anabaptist martyr (Zurich, 1527) was Felix Manz, the associate of Conrad Grebel, who is generally accredited as founding the movement. He pleaded before the Council of Zurich against the use of force to suppress those who rejected infant baptism. Though he lost his life, Manz and his fellow believers launched Christians on the long trek toward full religious liberty, almost three centuries distant. "In 1523–25, at Zurich, are the crossroads from which two roads lead down through history: the road of the free church of committed Christians separated from the state, with full religious liberty; and the road of the state church, territorially fixed, depending on state support, and forcibly suppressing all divergence, the road of intolerance and persecution."[3]

Calvin was not above using the state to punish heretics, even to death as in the case of Servetus. But even his good friend Nicholas Zurkinden, a member of the council of Bern that passed one such death sentence, rebelled inwardly at this kind of travesty.

Writing to Calvin years afterward, he said: "I freely confess that I also am one of those who desire to see the sword used as seldom as possible as a means of compulsion upon the opponents of the faith: and I am moved not so much by the Scripture passages which are cited, to keep the edge of the sword away from the treatment of matters of faith, as the unbelievable examples which have occurred in our time in the punishment of the Anabaptists. I was witness here when an eighty-year-old grandmother and her daughter, a mother of six children, were led to their death for no other reason than that they rejected infant baptism in accord with the well-known and common teaching of the Anabaptists."[4] He testifies to an historical reality which can be repeatedly demonstrated: once the sword is allowed in defense of religion there is no limit to injustice and tyranny. No liberty is safe where there is no freedom of religion.

We will look presently at the bases of religious freedom, but it is well to note the six grounds of such advocacy by Anabaptists as discerned by Bender: (1) the teaching and spirit of Christ expressly forbids any use of force; (2) the principle of voluntary church membership; (3) the Christian life as active discipleship rather than passive acceptance of the grace of God mediated through the Church; (4) the primacy of Christian love, even to one's enemies; (5) the way to victory through suffering; (6) faith as a gift from God that cannot be compelled by man.[5]

2. *Early Baptist Witness in Europe and America.* It has been noted above that present-day Baptists have no direct connection in origin with Anabaptists. But the early leaders, John Smyth and Thomas Helwys, were strongly influenced by their teachings. In "A Short Confession of Faith" the Helwys party in 1610 stated that in contrast to the Old Covenant Christ took away "also the kingly office, kingdom, sword, revenge appointed by the law" from the domain of the Church.[6] Furthermore, God has armored the Church only with spiritual weapons for the spiritual warfare. "And they being the redeemed of the Lord, who dwell in the house of the Lord, upon the Mount Sion, do change their fleshly weapons, namely, their swords into shares, and their spears into scythes, do lift up no sword, neither hath nor consent to fleshly battle."[7] In the context of their persecution by the authorities, both Catholic and Reformed, their first stand for liberty had to be directed against the Church. By this they disputed

107

the age-old concept of the two swords, the temporal and the spiritual, both under the control of the Church, which was Catholic doctrine. On the other side they disputed the Reformers' concept of the two orders, where the Church is superior to the State and has the right to use the latter for the defense of the faith.

Roger Williams, the founder of the colony of Rhode Island, has been called "the attending physician" for the birth of full religious liberty in any modern state.[8] His banishment from the Massachusetts Bay Colony was based upon these particular views: (1) The Church and the State cannot be co-extensive, for the Church is made up alone of the regenerate. There is no such thing as a Christian state. Citizenship ought not to be restricted to the regenerate, nor should the ideals of the Church be lowered to include all the populace. The sword belongs to the State for "civil vengeance and punishment"; the Word, as the sword of the Spirit, belongs to the Church for "spiritual vengeance and punishment." (2) Constraint of a man's conscience cannot but produce hypocrisy and so divine wrath. His repentance is an expedient which deludes both the man and his judges and results in a deceived conscience. (3) The erroneous conscience must be respected with the same freedom as the true. The end result may be a more moral and considerate life than that of an enforced yet true conscience. Given the diversity and fallibility of men, who is qualified to judge the conscience finally but God himself?

Williams was accused of opening the door to a great increase of "papists." The breadth of his soul, educated in a strict Calvinism, is nowhere better seen than in this statement, which could be thought very modern:

> ... if any or many conscientiously turn papists: I allege the experience of a holy, wise, and learned man, experienced in our own and other states' affairs, who affirms that he knew but few papists increase, where much liberty to papists was granted, yea, fewer than where they were restrained: Yet further, that in his conscience and judgment he believed and observed that such persons as conscientiously turned papists (as believing popery the truer way to heaven and salvation)—I say, such persons were ordinarily more conscionable, loving, and peace-

able in their dealings, and nearer to heaven than thousands that follow a bare common trade and road and name of Protestant religion, and yet live without all life of conscience and devotion to God, and consequently with as little love and faithfulness unto men.[9]

In our pride of the "founding fathers of our nation" it is easy to forget that with few exceptions the early colonists, who were escaping political and religious tyrannies of Europe, were hardly more liberal in their foundations than the countries they left. Though the Plymouth Colony was more open at first, soon all of New England came under the intolerance of the Massachusetts Bay Colony. Virginia and the Carolinas established the Anglican faith, and as late as the Revolution Baptists were still being imprisoned and fined for preaching and conducting assemblies. Peter Stuyvesant in New York established the Dutch Reformed Church until the English took over and changed to the Anglican faith. There both Baptists and Quakers were subject to arrest, whipping and banishment.

Maryland and Pennsylvania were remarkable exceptions. Lord Baltimore, a convert to Catholicism, established the colony of Maryland in 1632 and gave freedom of conscience to Protestant and Catholic alike. His "Toleration Act" of 1649, however, proscribed those guilty of blasphemy, denial of the Trinity, or reproaching Mary or the apostles. But by 1688 the tables had turned and the Protestant legislature repealed the Act of Toleration, forbade Catholic worship and even refused admission for Catholics to the colony. William Penn, the Quaker, opened his colony to all, only restricting public offices to those who professed faith in Christ. Only Rhode Island in its charter of 1663 guaranteed full liberty to all with no political hindrances to any on the basis of religion.[10]

3. *The Baptist Influence for the Bill of Rights.* When the colonies began to write their own constitutions after the Declaration of Independence, Virginia and Massachusetts opened the way for full guarantees of religious liberty in the new republic. Both were strongly influenced by Baptist leaders. In Virginia the political leaders, George Washington, James Madison, Thomas Jefferson and George Mason, were guided by the tenets of Deism and the social contract theory of John Locke. In 1776 under their

109

leadership the Virginia legislature adopted a constitution and passed a bill of rights. One of the latter, written by Mason, originally read: "That religion, or the duty which we owe to our Creator, and the manner of discharging it, can be directed only by reason and conviction, not by force or violence, and therefore all men are equally entitled to *tolerance* according to the dictates of conscience...."[11] Madison led the assembly to substitute *free exercise of religion* for *tolerance*. Still, John Leland and his Baptist cohorts were not satisfied that full liberty was theirs until the State was officially separated from the Anglican Church. Their fears were justified when Patrick Henry in 1784 introduced a bill that would provide a general tax for the equal support of every religious body.[12] The General Committee of Virginia Baptists led a strong attack against the bill. Still it might have passed had it not been for the powerful "Memorial and Remonstrance" of James Madison before the assembly. Among many reasons he brought against the bill we note here principles which have been appealed to many times since.

"Because it is proper to take alarm at the first experiment on our liberties." This has been called "the nose of the camel under the tent." While it can produce such a rigid view of separation of Church and State as to deny the influence of either upon the other, it yet proclaims the necessity of "eternal vigilance in the affairs of liberty."

"Who does not see that the same authority which can establish Christianity in exclusion of all other religions may establish with the same ease any particular sect of Christians in exclusion of all other sects? That the same authority which can force a citizen to contribute three pence only of his property for the support of any one establishment may force him to conform to any other establishment in all cases whatsoever." This states that when favoritism is shown in tax-support to one religious system, there is no barrier to unlimited favoritism, even if in justice the attempt were made to benefit all equally.

"Because experience witnesses that ecclesiastical establishments, instead of maintaining the purity and efficacy of religion, have had a contrary operation...." Now this is Madison's personal judgment, of course, but it is at one with the Baptist experience throughout history of having to break with both State and

Church in order to restore what they believed to be the purity of the Christian faith.

"Because the policy of the bill is adverse to the diffusion of the light of Christianity. . ."[13] It has long been a Baptist contention, joined by many others, that in a free, pluralistic state Christianity enjoys more vitality and growth because it must make its way through witness and persuasion of those without and by sole support of its own constituents.

"Because, finally, 'the equal right of every citizen to the free exercise of his religion according to the dictates of conscience' is held by the same tenure with all our other rights." Now Baptists have not tried to argue this principle as much as simply to hold it as axiomatic. This is justified by the very fact that the eventual Bill of Rights of the Constitution began with the guarantee of freedom of religion and tied it immediately in the same sentence with the other basic freedoms of speech, assembly, and petition:

Congress shall make no law respecting an establishment of religion, or prohibiting the free exercise thereof; or abridging the freedom of speech, or of the press; or the right of the people peaceably to assemble and to petition the Government for a redress of grievances.

Isaac Backus, a Baptist leader, presented a plea for a religious liberty clause to the Massachusetts delegation to the Continental Congress of 1774. It was not until the fight to ratify the new Constitution, however, that religious liberty was finally a political reality for the Republic. Virginia was a key state in that struggle. The Baptists of that state were about to put up their leader against the powerful James Madison as delegate to the Convention on Ratification. John Leland had written a long letter to Madison spelling out ten objections to the Constitution unless a bill of rights was adopted. Madison visited the Baptist leader and under the trees at his farm home the latter agreed to throw the weight of Virginia Baptists behind Madison for his assurance that he would introduce such a bill in the coming convention.[14] The bill as finally written by Thomas Jefferson was adopted in 1789 and ratified by the states two years later.

Merrimon Cuninggim summarizes the role of the little people in this struggle for liberty of conscience:

> Both the Bill of Rights and the Statute of Religious Freedom were enacted through the generalship of Madison and his helpers, with Jefferson playing the strategist's role; but the privates in the ranks were the dissenters. And if there had been no large and determined army there would have been no fight. The victory for religious liberty was a compound of many forces, the work of many diverse people, the outgrowth of many varied movements. But that one element that could not possibly have been spared, that one factor more effective than any of the rest, was the participation of the dissenting Protestants.[15]

4. *Continuing Struggle for Religious Liberty in America.* As is so often the case with human movements, once liberty was guaranteed by the Constitution many concluded the victory was permanent and there need be no further concern. But it was not to be so. It took until 1833 when the last state, Massachusetts, finally completed the disestablishment of any church. Soon the problem arose from an unexpected quarter. "Though legally disestablished, the churches (sadly including Baptists) often acted as if there was a sort of general Protestant establishment and sought to use legislation to enforce their view of morality upon the nation. They dipped occasionally into the public treasury for support of their work and held on to an older privileged position. It took greater courage perhaps to oppose, as many did, such subtle abuses of church-state separation than to act when the issues had been clear cut."[16] The great migrations, mostly of Catholic peoples from Europe and Ireland, in the eighteenth century aroused such anti-Catholic fears as to attract many Baptists to nativistic movements. Some of these were tempted to deny the rights of citizens or to restrict them seriously in their antagonisms. Gradually also Baptists sought political means to enforce with other Protestants such characteristic moral codes as the Puritan sabbath (to the disadvantage of Jews and Seventh-Day adherents), temperance, and book censorship.

B. A LOOK AT THE BASES OF RELIGIOUS LIBERTY

We have been tracing the way Baptists have been shaped by, and the contributions they have made to, the cause of religious liberty. By no means should any conclude that Baptists are the dominant force in this cause. Practically all Protestants, and since Vatican II Catholics also, are caught up in these concerns. Not only are all concerned for religious liberty in such communist countries as Russia and Muslim states as Iran and Turkey, but even in the United States the problem has taken on the greatest complexity. In the last generation the State has entered through education and welfare programs fields that once belonged solely to the churches. All of this and more calls for the profoundest study of the philosophical, religious and legal bases of liberty, civil and religious, economic and personal.

It is beyond the scope of this book and much more the capability of its author to attempt more than a brief look, first at some definitions and distinctions, and then at some biblical and theological grounds.

1. *Definitions and Distinctions.* A good place to start is the distinction between *tolerance* and religious *liberty* drawn by the eminent Jesuit scholar, John Courtney Murray. As one of the *periti* at the Second Vatican Council he was largely responsible for the writing of the Declaration on Religious Freedom. He describes the long-standing policy of tolerance of the Catholic Church:

> The theory of religious tolerance takes its start from the statement, considered to be axiomatic, that error has no rights, that only the truth has rights, and exclusive rights. From this axiom a juridical theory is deduced, which distinguishes between "thesis" and "hypothesis." The thesis asserts that Catholicism, *per se* and in principle, should be established as the one "religion of the state since it is the one true religion." Given the institution of establishment, it follows by logical and juridical consequence that no other religion, *per se* and in principle, can be allowed public existence or action within the state. . . . Error has no rights. Therefore error is to be suppressed whenever and wherever possible; intolerance is the rule. Error, however, may be tolerated

113

when tolerance is necessary by reason of circumstances, that is, when intolerance is impossible; tolerance remains the exception.[17]

Now this is obviously not religious freedom, for a tolerance, when exercised either by a dominant church or by an all-powerful state, has no respect for the validity and autonomy of a contrary religion. Rights which are offered only in sufferance can be revoked for cause. Religious liberty exists on the contrary only when it is inalienable and irrevocable.

Freedom implies the absence of restraint; liberty is the wider, more positive license to accomplish aims and so fulfill the nature of man and his religious societies. Religious liberty is an inclusive concept. It begins with the individual in freedom of conscience. This is a concern of the Church, for in its evangelizing, educating and disciplining there must finally be room for the individual conscience to be free, else it is no longer moral. This is a concern of the State, for its laws and national policies must never abridge the free exercise of conscience. And this is pointedly demonstrated in the matter of conscientious objectors in the time of war.

Religious liberty extends from the individual to his religious group and grants freedom to assemble and to worship "according to the dictates of conscience." This includes again the freedom to witness and to propagate religion, restrained only by respect for the rights of others and the civil order of the State. True freedom exists only when the dominant religious group accepts responsibility for the freedom of its minorities. Where the State and the Church overlap, both have the responsibility of recognizing the legal and religious distinctions fostered by each.

2. *Theological bases of religious liberty.* Let us summarize our argument for religious liberty with these four theological considerations:

1. There is one God of all men. As creator and provider of all he shows partiality toward none (Matt. 5:45; Rom. 2:11; Acts 10:34–35). He "would have all men to be saved" (I Tim. 2:4), "not wishing that any should perish, but that all should come to repentance" (II Peter 3:9). He is not the God of peoples of a single race or a single religion (Rom. 3:29). He has ways of revealing himself that go beyond the Judaeo-Christian witnesses (Acts

14:17; Rom. 1:19–20; 2:14–15). This requires a respect and a sensitivity on the part of those witnesses to "the heathen" which too often are ignored or at best not sought after.

2. The dignity of man. As we have discussed the competency of the soul under the lordship of Christ, we need only call attention to the fundamental truths of the nature of man as human and as Christian.

3. The only power and authority granted to Christ's followers is that which he himself wielded. It is the power of the Cross: "And I, if I be lifted up from the earth, will draw all men unto myself" (John 12:32). He would persuade men through redeeming love. It is his word that "is living, and active, and sharper than any two-edged sword, and piercing even to the dividing of soul and spirit, of both joints and marrow and quick to discern the thoughts and intents of the heart" (Heb. 4:12).

4. The sole motive and operating power, then, is that of *agape* love. The church has no other force. The State, without such resource, is shut up to the operation of laws, which can frequently show injustice and even coercion. But the Church can only take it patiently and fight back with the weapons of the Spirit, clothed with "the whole armor of God"—truth, righteousness, peace, and faith (Eph. 6:11–18).

C. THE PROBLEMS OF THE "WALL OF SEPARATION"

All of the foregoing discussion of religious liberty may lead some to assume that we only have to write the guarantee of religious liberty into the constitution and laws of any land in order to secure permanent freedom. Such is far from the case. The United States has not only been the pioneer, but the chief exemplar of religious liberty for all modern states. We have the pluralism of peoples, cultures, and religions to undergird a doctrine of fairness to all and of unity through diversity. All Protestant bodies are on record in support of the Bill of Rights. Now as a result of the Declaration on Religious Freedom of the Second Vatican Council the Roman Catholic Church is also strongly committed (see below). Champions of religious liberty have been able to rely largely upon the decisions of the U.S. Supreme Court. Nevertheless, in no other country has there been so much agonizing over the interpretation and applications. Many have concluded that so long as human societies, both political and religious, remain fallible, there can be no rest from this struggle.

Much appeal to the cause has been based upon Thomas Jefferson's famous phrase, "a wall of separation between church and State." It is well to quote him in the context of his reply as President to a letter of commendation from the Danbury Baptist Association in Connecticut in 1802:

> Believing with you that religion is a matter which lies solely between man and his God, that he owes account to none other for his faith or his worship, that the legislative powers of government reach actions only, and not opinions, I contemplate with sovereign reverence that act of the whole American people which declared that their legislature should "make no law respecting an establishment of religion, or prohibiting the free exercise thereof," thus building *a wall of separation between church and State.* Adhering to this expression of the supreme will of the nation in behalf of the rights of conscience, I shall see with sincere satisfaction the progress of those sentiments which tend to restore to man all his natural rights, convinced he has *no natural right in opposition to his social duties.*[18]

Now some have argued that by the figure of the "wall" the founding fathers of the country never intended for a hard and fast separation that would ignore that both Church and State operate in the same realm of the social life of its people. The last clause of the quotation above would seem to bear this out. Jefferson may have been overly optimistic in concluding that man has "no natural right in opposition to his social duties." With the careful delineations of a limited state which he held, he could not foresee the modern concern of the State for the same welfare and just causes which have long been the preserve of religion.

Glenn Hinson has located three areas where "the taut line" of separation has been difficult to define: (1) State aid to religion, both direct for denominational educational and welfare institutions, and indirect aid, such as tax exemption of Church property; (2) Church involvement in State affairs, by seeking legislative recourse for moral concerns such as temperance, anti-pornography, Sabbath laws, and abortion disputes; (3) State involvement in Church affairs, such as court settlements of Church property disputes, application of equal opportunity laws, and the appointment of an ambassador or representative to the Vatican.

Much Protestant-Catholic tension has arisen over State aid to education. Protestants have tended to justify Bible reading and prayer in the public schools, released time for religious instruction, baccalaureate services and non-denominational departments of religion in state colleges and universities. Catholics have generally defended State aid to parochial schools, the incorporation of a parochial school into a public system, garbed nuns teaching in public schools, and, where full direct aid has not been allowed by the Supreme Court, financial support for textbooks, bus transportation, and school lunches. Both Protestants and Catholics have been in substantial agreement on the legitimacy of chaplains in the military and state institutions, tax exemption for religious property and activities, and social security for the clergy.

Classic Supreme Court cases have been occasioned by specific problems presented by certain religious groups in America. In the last century the Mormons precipitated a crisis over polygamy. In this century the Jehovah's Witnesses have been before the Court several times on their stand against saluting the flag and transfusion of blood. The Amish have withstood the State over enforced education of their children. Sabbatarians have struggled against the Sunday "blue laws." More recently the members of the Unification Church ("Moonies") have provoked decisions over their claim to freedom to witness in public places. The Church of Scientology and some lesser groups have exercised the courts sorely over the problem of the legal definitions of religion. The Justice branch may no longer be able to assume those definitions provided by religious bodies as in earlier years.

This brief listing of the areas of overlap and tension barely opens the window upon the complexities of the interpretation and applications of the principle of the "separation of Church and State." It should be obvious by now that strict separation is an ideal which is both impossible and unwise, for it would deny the prophetic voice of the Church to criticize the State, and the "social duties" of Christians in the exercise of their religious practices.

Hinson argues for a clear distinction together with "mutual helpfulness" between Church and State. He urges no favoritism of any particular religious body by the State and does not believe that the American policy should lead to the "total secularization of the state."[19] He points out that "the health and survival of soul liberty depend on the maintenance of delicate balances." These he defines as the State's balance between hostility and control and that of favoritism; the Church's balance between freedom of propagating its faith and the rights of others, between missionary zeal and respect for human conscience. Liberty of conscience cannot finally be denied, as countless martyrs to the faith have attested. Liberty of religion is a freedom that must continually be won through the exercise of justice on the part of the State and love by the Church. Anything less is an ultimate denial of the one God who is father and judge of all mankind.[20]

D. THE DECLARATION ON RELIGIOUS LIBERTY OF THE SECOND VATICAN COUNCIL

No contemporary discussion of religious liberty would be complete without acknowledging the tremendous contribution of the Catholic Church at the recent Council. Together with the Decree of Ecumenism, which for the first time in history formally recognized "the separated Churches and communities," the Declaration on Religious Liberty opened an entirely new era in the history of religious freedom. Even before the final passage of the Declaration, December 7, 1965, Pope John XXIII had called Cardinal Bea to establish the Papal Commission on Christian Unity. It is significant that two Americans played a strong role in the delicate politics of the Council in helping to bring about the Declaration. John Courtney Murray, S.J., a *peritus* (theological consultant), has been recognized widely as most influential, even to the final written form of the document.[21] The other was a young Paulist Father, Thomas Stransky, who later as president of his order of missionary priests has been very active in ecumenical dialogues. He served in the Commission on Christian Unity under Cardinal Bea and his successor, Cardinal Willebrands.

The Declaration defines religious freedom thus: "This freedom means that all men are to be immune from coercion on the part of individuals or of social groups and of any human power, in such wise that in matters religious no one is to be forced to act in a manner contrary to his own beliefs."[22] Murray identifies two aspects in this and points to the new element: "First, no man is to be forced to act in a manner contrary to his personal beliefs; second, no man is to be forcibly restrained from acting in accordance with his beliefs. The affirmation of this latter immunity is the new thing, which is in harmony with the older affirmation of the former immunity."[23] This freedom from coercion for the individual is enlarged to include his religious community in paragraph 4. This is spelled out in terms of freedom of assembly and worship, the right to educate children and establish religious institutions, particularly seminaries, and freedom for missionary endeavor. The Council recognized the right of the State to set norms for social order and of Christians to obey its laws, but without hindrance from the government in the exercise of religion. Government is urged "to help create conditions favorable to the fostering of religious life,"[24] but these are not spelled out.

Baptists, who among others have felt the lash of Catholic persecution in the past, rejoice at the tremendous stride toward full religious freedom made here by the Catholic Church. Even though only one sentence in the Declaration admits the former intolerance—"In the life of the People of God as it has made its pilgrim way through the vicissitudes of human history, there have at times appeared ways of acting which were less in accord with the spirit of the gospel and even opposed to it"[25]—the Declaration taken in its entirety is a humble about-face for the once triumphalistic Church.

Still, we could wish that the Church had gone farther. There is no disavowal of the right of the Church to be established in a State wherever possible. Instead the Church is urged to be tolerant of minorities: "If, in view of peculiar circumstances obtaining among certain peoples, special legal recognition is given in the constitutional order of society to one religious body, it is at the same time imperative that the right of all citizens and religious bodies to religious freedom should be recognized and made effective in practice."[26]

The Declaration is concerned chiefly with the freedom for the exercise of religion of the Church itself in those countries where the government might be alien or hostile. It has nothing to say about the freedom for dissent within its own ranks, and

119

this has led to much confusion in the development of religious renewal in the years since. It is agreed that both here and elsewhere in the *Documents,* final appeal is made by the individual to his conscience before God. But in the light of the claim that the Church is the custodian of truth, both that which is revealed and "those principles of the moral order which have their origin in human nature itself,"[27] it is not likely that the Catholic conscience is ever going to be finally free to pursue Truth apart from its authoritative teachers.

Philip Wogaman expressed the basic cause of a limited approval of the Church's Declaration:

> While there is no reason to doubt the sincerity of the new generation of Catholic political thinkers or the good faith of the church in adopting its basically progressive Declaration on Religious Liberty, it may yet be said that the basis still remains upon which the older claims of dogmatic intolerance were previously made. I am thinking of the claim that the Catholic Church is the repository of absolute religious truth and objectively valid means of grace, in relation to which other religious claims are relatively in error, and of the hierarchical system which remains for the authoritative interpretation of doctrine. . . . If modern Catholicism is still understood to possess infallibility in dogma and objective means of grace, identified with institutional forms and administered by an authoritative priesthood and hierarchy, does there not remain a logical basis for political efforts to further the church in its objectively valid mission and to impede competitive efforts insofar as circumstances of time and place permit? . . . One may believe the question to be largely academic in the present spirit of ecumenicity, but at the same time one may continue to hope for further modifications of the doctrine of the Church.[28]

In spite of sharing Wogaman's criticism, this author agrees that the Council has ushered in a new day in which there is much possibility for cooperation between Catholic, Protestant and Jew in the cause of liberty of religion world wide. It is just as true here as in other areas: so long as religious liberty does not truly exist in any country of the world, no country can rest secure with its own measure of freedom. Perhaps the ultimate battle is against that weakness of human nature so poignantly described by Milton,

> Than to love Bondage more than Liberty,
> Bondage with ease than strenuous liberty.[29]

NOTES

1. Robert A. Baker, ed., *A Baptist Source Book* (Nashville: Baptist Press, 1966), p. 40.

2. *Ibid.*, pp. 41–42.

3. Harold S. Bender, *The Anabaptists and Religious Liberty in the Sixteenth Century* (Philadelphia: Fortress Press, 1970), p. 8.

4. *Ibid.*, p. 18.

5. *Ibid.*, p. 19.

6. *Op. cit.*, p. 105.

7. *Ibid.*, p. 107.

8. Glenn Hinson, *Soul Liberty* (Nashville: Convention Press, 1975), p. 96.

9. Roland H. Bainton, *The Travail of Religious Liberty* (Philadelphia: The Westminster Press, 1951), p. 223.

10. I am indebted to Hinson, *op. cit.*, pp. 90–98, for this summary.

11. Baker, *op. cit.*, pp. 34–35; italics mine.

12. This system still prevails in West Germany and certain other European countries.

13. All quotes are from Baker, *op. cit.*, pp. 36–37.

14. The story is told in full by O. K. and Marjorie Armstrong, *The Indomitable Baptists* (Garden City: Doubleday and Co., 1967), pp. 8–16.

15. Merrimon Cuninggim, *Freedom's Holy Light* (New York: Harper and Brothers, 1955), pp. 106–107.

16. Pope A. Duncan, "Baptists and Other Denominations," *Baptist Advance* (Nashville: Broadman Press, 1964), p. 391.

17. John Courtney Murray, S.J. ed., *Freedom and Man* (New York: P. J. Kennedy and Sons, 1965), p. 134.

18. A. F. Carrillo de Albornoz, *The Basis of Religious Liberty* (New York: Association Press, 1963), p. 44.

19. H. A. Washington, ed., *The Writings of Thomas Jefferson,* Vol. 8 (New York: Derby and Jackson, 1859), p. 113.

20. Hinson, *op. cit.*, pp. 106–107.

21. For more detailed discussion of the issues involved in the application of the principle of separation, see Leo Pfeffer, *Church, State, and Freedom* (Boston: Beacon Press, 1967); Philip Wogamon, *Protestant Faith and Religious Liberty* (Nashville: Abingdon Press, 1967); Glenn T. Miller, *Religious Liberty in America* (Philadelphia: The Westminster Press), 1976.

22. See the symposiums edited by John Courtney Murray, S.J., which deal with the many issues: *Freedom and Man* (New York: P. J. Kennedy and Sons, 1965), and *Religious Liberty: An End and a Beginning* (New York: The Macmillan Co., 1966).

23. Number 2, Murray's translation in *Religious Liberty: An End and a Beginning* (New York: The Macmillan Co., 1966).

24. *Ibid.*, footnote 4, p. 166.)

25. *Ibid.*

26. *Ibid.*

27. *Ibid.*

28. Wogaman, *op. cit.*, pp. 39–40.

29. *Samson Agonistes,* 11. 270–271.

chapter nine

WE ARE BECOMING
SOCIALLY AWARE

In 1920 the annual meeting of the Baptists of Virginia made the following statement which was characteristic of Southern Baptists from their founding: "The Baptist attitude towards all social reform work and service is that *the unadulterated gospel preached and accepted* solves all social problems, rightly adjusts all industrial inequalities, removes domestic frictions, adjourns divorce courts and supplies adequate protection and uplift to the weaker part of humanity."[1]

In 1975 Broadman Press, the official publisher of the Southern Baptist Sunday School Board, published the book, *Applying the Gospel*, "Suggestions for Christian Social Action in a Local Church." Written by the then professor of Christian Ethics of Southwestern Baptist Theological Seminary, it was sponsored by the Christian Life Commission of the Southern Baptist Convention as "an invaluable book for church leaders." In his introduction William Pinson says:

With the Bible as our guide, Christians need to become as concerned about dirty air and water as we have been about dirty books and movies. We need to become as concerned about the immoral use of sex in marriage for irresponsible procreation as we have been about it apart from marriage in fornication. We need to become as concerned about people who are kept out of Baptist churches because of race as we have been about those let in without benefit of Baptist immersion. We need to become as concerned about what the poor have for supper as we have been about who is eligible to partake of the Lord's Supper. This we must do if we are true to the Bible.[2]

Now we must not conclude that Pinson represents the majority of Southern Baptists in his passionate advocacy of Christian social action. But the fact that his book was published with such sponsorship indicates that Southern Baptists have come a long way in social awareness. What are some reasons for this changed attitude?

1. *Critical reflections on some basic assumptions.* It is clear that Pinson does not accept the broad statement that "the unadulterated gospel preached and accepted solves all social problems." It is unrealistic to believe that a gospel designed primarily for individual regeneration is, *ipso facto,* applicable to the evils entrenched in social institutions. It is overly optimistic to hold that congregations will "accept" for long the kind of prophetic preaching of the gospel that condemns its cherished cultural mores. Finally, it is wishful thinking to trust even "changed lives" to solve social ills apart from concerted action directed at their causes. Those Baptists who are doing this kind of critical thinking have also recognized that Baptist bodies have never refrained from engaging in direct political and social action when the issue was one of personal or family morality, such as temperance, gambling, and divorce. It is inconsistent then to cry "politics" or "social gospel" when it is a matter of racial or economic injustice.

One of the pioneers in this kind of critical evaluation, J. M. Dawson, held that "much of the evangelism to which people are exposed is incapable of inspiring brotherhood and solving social problems. This incapacity is due to the limited appeal of evangelism. Some preachers put a larger emphasis upon justification than upon regeneration. The result is a people who have faith in justification without the experience of regeneration. Their main business is to get to heaven. They continue in their insensitivity to any moral obligation to change unrighteous social conditions because they are the products of an evangelism which has not drawn upon the prophetic tradition of Christianity."[3]

2. *Cultural change.* The South is no longer "solid" politically and Southern Baptists are less "southern" than before World

War II. That war caused great migrations of Baptists to non-southern states, whereas before they had been largely confined to the eighteen states of the South and Southwest. Postwar industrialization in the South brought large migrations of people from the North and Midwest. Southern Baptists are now in all fifty states, and the once all-southern congregations in the newer states are giving way to indigenous members and pastors. The growing number of ethnic churches is leavening the Convention with their social concerns. The invasion of the State into all areas of human welfare and service, formerly the preserve of the Church, has made impossible a strict separation of the Christian as church member and as citizen. With more and more welfare programs of the State, there is less emphasis upon denominational institutions of hospitals, orphanages, and other remedial and custodial ministries. In their place has come a new concern for the moral quality and just measures of the State in its functions.

Southern Baptists are increasingly aware of our cultural conditioning throughout our history. Even the limited contacts with other Baptist bodies in the Baptist World Alliance and our own language missions have helped to distinguish between what is Christian and deservedly Baptist from what is only Southern.

3. *A generation of socially aware leaders among Southern Baptists.* Authority among Baptists allows only leadership by moral suasion and spiritual example. There can be no Pope Leo XIII setting forth social principles as in an encyclical like *Rerum Novarum* (1891). The resolutions passed annually at Baptist conventions cannot have upon the churches the impact of a Vatican Council in its Constitution on the Church in the Modern World. Social progress may be slower, but Baptist polity generally keeps its leadership closer to the growing edge of lay involvement than in those denominations capable of juridical decrees.

In the light of this, some critics even within the denomination, have been frustrated with the slow growth of social concern of Southern Baptists. But there have been forces at work that are remarkable in the light of Baptist history. Four of these deserve appreciation. The Christian Life Commission of the Convention has set the pace for Baptists in a rising social consciousness. The Home Mission Board has pioneered in Christian social ministries, aided greatly by the action groups of the Woman's Missionary Union and more recently by the Baptist Men's organization. For more than a generation the six seminaries have had able and courageous men teaching social ethics to future pastors and denominational leaders. Finally, there have been a few pioneers, often ostracized, who have dared a radical social application of the Gospel.

A. A LOOK BACKWARD FROM WHENCE WE HAVE COME

Southern Baptists organized their Convention in 1845 over a social issue that divided other denominations also. That does not mean that they were in principle dedicated to the social application of the Gospel. Strongly influenced by pietism with its focus upon private religion, they were caught up in the great revival movements of the frontier. Largely a rural people with uneducated pastors they were untouched by the theological movements which produced the "social gospel" in the latter part of the nineteenth century. They were suspicious of liberalism and so early tagged the social gospel as being subversive of individual regeneration.

These were the guiding principles of the early period. Responsibility for public morals rests primarily upon the individual Christian citizen. Social change comes about only through changed lives, through the new birth. Private morality is the chief focus of preaching and family discipline. Churches and denominations are not to engage in partisan politics, except, of course, where great moral issues are at stake. The chief contribution of churches is the remedial ministry to the victims of social ills: orphanages, hospitals, homes for unwed mothers and juvenile delinquents. Even though the editors of state papers seldom hesitated to express their views on every moral, political and social issue of their day, still the nature of Baptist polity and the lack of strong denominational loyalty in that era prevented any concerted action by Southern Baptists on any issue except temperance.[4]

Through the Civil War Baptist editors were able to give biblical justification of slavery. Baptists were the most successful in evangelizing the Negro because of their emphasis upon personal regeneration and the hope of a better world to come. Eighmy points out the irony of their success:

126

Masters usually welcomed Baptist preaching, which stressed an other-wordly hope and personal morality, because such teaching did more to strengthen than to undermine the slave system. Those who preached to the slave population were fully conscious of such practical considerations. One minister, in an appeal for the support of work among the slaves, calculated that conversion would increase the value of slaves by more than 10 percent.[5]

The Reconstruction Period with its racial bitterness led the Negro Baptists to form their own congregations and later conventions. These became the chief source of social identity and human refuge that eventually provided the civil rights movement of the 1960's with its leadership and power.

It was the temperance movement that laid the foundation of later Baptist involvement in social concerns. Prior to the latter half of the nineteenth century Baptists had everywhere preached moderation but seldom total abstinence. As the frontier expanded westward the evils of liquor took its increasing toll upon personal and family life. With the law sore pressed to stem the tide of criminal activity, the churches provided the only bulwark of morality, even of justice, in interpersonal affairs. The shield of temperance seemed the most available recourse in the struggle. It provided a clear-cut answer for every individual and family and societal group. It could be defended biblically and it provided a worthy cause around which otherwise divided Protestants could readily unite. The early champions of the "social gospel" also made temperance their foremost concern.

In the latter half of the nineteenth century Baptist conventions were urging their members to support the Woman's Christian Temperance Union, the Anti-Saloon leagues and the budding prohibition movement. A Temperance Committee was formed by the 1910 Southern Baptist Convention with A. J. Barton as chairman. In early reports to the Convention Barton urged Baptists to become involved in every aspect of concern for social ills, primarily, though, with a view to the support of temperance.

The first Social Service Commission was formed in 1911 by the Georgia Baptist Convention. E. C. Dargan, its founder and chairman, showed a wide range of social interests including poverty, labor relations, political corruption and criminal justice. In the same year there was a call at the Baptist World Alliance for a committee on social progress to work with like committees of other denominations.

In 1913 the Southern Convention established a Social Service Commission with W. L. Poteat, president of Wake Forest College in North Carolina, as chairman. Two years later this was merged with the Temperance Committee under Barton's leadership. His importance in the social consciousness of Southern Baptists during a whole generation is stated by Welton Gaddy:

> He personally dominated the Social Service and Temperance Committee writing every one of its reports as well as every report of the [succeeding] Social Service Commission up until 1942. His dominant concern for the anti-liquor movement was readily accepted by Southern Baptists. Only after some time as leader of the Committee did he attempt to move it and the Convention into a consideration of other social issues.[5]

At times he could evidence a broader concern: "So long as there is social inequality, industrial injustice, or political crime, the Kingdom of God is not fully come, and you and I have a message and a mission."[6] Specific mention was made of sweat shops, child labor, prostitution, tenant problems and political corruption. Proposals were offered, however, only for action in the field of temperance. When World War I involved the United States, Barton urged war-time ministries, but no judgment on the war itself.

In 1920, with national prohibition assured, the report to the Convention for the first time took note of the needs of the Negro population. Segregation was assumed without mention. Better education, housing, employment opportunities, and justice in the courts were the emphases. Cooperation was urged with interracial committees to cultivate understanding.

Barton's methodology is clear in his 1933 report to the Convention: "Society is to be saved through the salvation of the individual; social service is not in any sense or to any degree a substitute for individual personal regeneration and salvation."[8]

Frequently the Commission followed cultural attitudes rather than challenging them. In the years of peace, war was denounced and peace treaties and movements encouraged. The 1932 report favored "the renunciation of war, the reduction of armaments and the development of internal institutions such as the World Court, for the peaceful settlement of controversies between nations."[9] But the 1940 report justified a "purely defensive war" and urged resistance to the Axis powers. Support for the war was immediately forthcoming after Pearl Harbor. The Convention did recognize the right of conscientious objectors and provided a means for registering them.

In the 1930's the Social Service Commission broadened its interests, while continually urging a return to prohibition, at least of the local option variety. There were increasing pronouncements on issues of Church and State, particularly on the matter of a diplomatic representative to the Vatican. The Vatican State was never recognized as other than the religious headquarters of world Catholicism. Hence to send a representative is to acknowledge the temporal power of the papacy and provide a governmental link with one religion over all others. This in Baptist eyes was the "nose of the camel under the tent" which could lead to the establishment of the Catholic religion in America (and elsewhere) in defiance of the First Amendment to the Constitution.

Other concerns of the 1930's were race relations, divorce laws, gambling, ballroom dancing, and salacious movies. A farreaching move of this year was the launching of Christian Life Conferences annually at the Southern Baptist Assembly, Ridgecrest, North Carolina.

In 1933 Edwin McNeill Poteat, a nephew of President W. L. Poteat, and a North Carolina pastor, sought to lead the Convention to establish a Social Research Agency. At the time Barton's Commission had no paid staff and was limited to its annual reports and the articles Barton wrote for state papers. Poteat's acknowledged liberal stand in theology and ethics caused fear among many that the Southern Baptist Convention would be drawn into the Social Gospel Movement. The proposal was tabled and killed in 1936. It was not until 1948 that the effort was resumed.

Gaddy evaluated the Barton era thus: "A. J. Barton had

moved Southern Baptists from their pre-twentieth century and pre-World War I stances to at least a recognition of several social problems and the formation of an agency to deal with them. Where Southern Baptists had said nothing in the past, they were now voicing opinions on social issues through their Social Service Commission."[10]

J. B. Weatherspoon became chairman of the Commission at Barton's death in 1943. He greatly expanded the philosophy and strategy of the Commission. His chief contribution was his effort to combine evangelism, education and ethics into a practical social action program. In 1947 he succeeded in getting the Southern Baptist Convention to fund the Commission and employ a professional staff. During his leadership growing attention was paid to race relations.

A. C. Miller became Executive Secretary of the Commission in 1953 and moved the office to Nashville. This brought the Commission into closer relationship with both the Executive Committee of the Convention and the nearby Sunday School Board. It greatly improved communication of its message to Baptists in the churches. At the instigation of T. B. Maston, Professor of Christian Ethics at Southwestern Baptist Theological Seminary, Fort Worth, the Convention changed the name to the Christian Life Commission. Miller sought to undergird social action with a broad biblical basis in a vastly expanded series of tracts and articles.

When the 1954 Supreme Court ruled on desegregating public schools, the Commission recommended and the Convention urged its people to support the peaceful implementation of the ruling. The Convention voted overwhelmingly, being the second religious body in America to announce public support. Then opposition arose. Miller observed that "great numbers of our people were aroused to hostility toward us because they had never known of the work of the Social Service Commission and felt that this Commission out of Nashville was something their leadership had fostered upon them to force the racial question down their throats."[11] But the Convention leadership stood by the Commission's stand. Miller attributed the survival of the Commission to the long-term effects of the teaching in the (then) three seminaries, the influence of the Woman's Missionary Union and the groundwork of the old Social Service Commission.

With this the die was cast and a new era of wider social responsibility among Southern Baptists was begun. In 1960 Foy D. Valentine became the Executive Secretary of the Christian Life Commission, coming from a like post at the Baptist General Convention of Texas. Under his leadership the Commission has greatly extended its scope, enlarged its staff to the present nine professionals, and helped to guide the Convention through the stormy years of the civil rights movement and the Vietnam War.

During the 1960's the Home Mission Board played a strategic role in the progress of Southern Baptists in social responsibility. For years it had pioneered in cooperative work with National Baptists under the direction of Guy Bellamy and Victor Glass. In 1965 the new Executive, Arthur Rutledge, led in the creation of two new departments of work: Christian Social Ministries, to provide skilled leadership to churches and associations in all kinds of ministry to people without regard to their race or religion, and the Department of Interfaith Witness, to aid Baptists in understanding and relating to peoples of all world religions.

While the nation flamed with racial tensions the Convention met in Houston in 1968. Glass and Rutledge felt Baptists must speak to the issues that were threatening to rend asunder the whole fabric of national life. They brought to the Convention an eleven hundred word statement, signed by seventy-one leaders of every agency, state convention leaders and editors. The statement acknowledged Baptists' responsibility: "Along with all other citizens we recognize our share of responsibility for creating in our land conditions in which justice, order and righteousness can prevail." It called for immediate focusing of the resources and influence of the denomination in effecting social change.

The Home Mission Board was given the role of leadership in implementing the statement. Executive Secretary Arthur Rutledge quickly called the leaders of thirteen Southern Baptist agencies together to map strategy. All avenues of communication were used to create a climate of reconciliation and practical ministry. Among other moves, the Mission Board assigned twenty-two college student summer missionaries to serve in the Watts area of Los Angeles, a grant was made to the Opportunities Industrialization Center of Philadelphia, a black self-help program, and a million-dollar loan fund was established for non-SBC black churches. All of this was not without strong opposition from certain churches, a few of which withdrew affiliation from the Convention. But with the crisis came a new commitment on the part of Southern Baptists in race relations. The first black director of any agency, Emmanuel McCall, now heads the Black Church Relations Department of the Home Mission Board. There are now over six hundred black churches affiliated with the Southern Baptist and state conventions and an estimated 3,780 other Southern Baptist churches with black members.

In 1978 the Christian Life Commission led the Convention in Atlanta to adopt a "Declaration of Human Rights" which urges among other things, "Let Southern Baptist churches be boldly involved in championing justice for the oppressed, providing food for the hungry, supporting changes in those laws and systems which abuse the poor while providing loopholes for the rich, doing the things that make for peace, and effecting change where change is needed to support basic human rights."

Eighmy has helped Southern Baptists realize their cultural conditioning. His conclusion is worth noting:

> Whether a democratic church can exercise loyalty to an authority that transcends its cultural environment remains an open question. But, as demonstrated by the civil rights controversy, when a question with clear moral implications demands commitments, Southern Baptists can be led to translate Christian principles into practical declarations.[12]

He expressed his hope for the future shortly before his untimely death: "The main source of hope is the ever-growing number of enlightened leaders who are vocal, influential, and strategically located in pastorates, schools, and denominational positions. For the character of Southern Baptist influence in the secular world will be determined largely by the extent to which leaders of this sort are allowed to shape denominational social attitudes and action."[13]

B. POSTSCRIPT TO CHAPTER IV

Many social issues are of growing concern to all Christians. The Christian Life Commission, which qualifies as nearly as any other agency of Southern Baptists as their social conscience, produces pamphlets and study guides for the use of pastors and churches. The range of issues treated by current literature of the Commission is quite revealing in the light of the history sketched above. The topics and number of separate pamphlets available (1980) are as follows:

Aging	4
Alcohol and Drugs	5
Citizenship	6
Ecology and Economics	6
Marriage, Family, Sex	24
Poverty and Hunger	2
War and Peace	6
Miscellaneous	3

For those who are interested in current pronouncement on these issues, Appendix I is taken from "A Statement of Social Principles for Christian Social Concern and Christian Social Action" issued by the Christian Life Commission in 1979. The Appendix contains that part of the "statement" which gives a brief summary of positions on every issue addressed in recent years by the Commission. It is important to note their conclusion: "This statement of social principles is provided *for* Baptists *concerned* about thinking biblically and acting responsibly in the arena of applied Christianity" [italics mine]. The italics indicate the Commission's self-understanding of its role. It does not try to speak *to* the churches authoritatively. It recognizes that not all Baptists agree with its stand. It sees itself rather as a resource agency and a catalyst "in the arena of applied Christianity."[14]

NOTES

1. Minutes of the Baptist General Association of Virginia, 1920. Italics mine.

2. William M. Pinson, Jr., *Applying the Gospel* (Nashville: Broadman Press, 1975), p. 11.

133

3. George D. Kelsey, *Social Ethics among Southern Baptists, 1917–1969* (Metuchen, N. J.: The Scarecrow Press, 1973), pp. 12–13.

4. Kelsey, *op. cit.,* relies upon state Baptist papers for voluminous quotes on the moral and social issues that concerned Southern Baptists up to 1969.

5. Eighmy, *op. cit.,* p. 25, referring to the Minutes, Alabama Baptist Convention, 1846, p. 18.

6. Curtis Welton Gaddy, "The Christian Life Commission of the Southern Baptist Convention: A Critical Evaluation" (unpublished Ph.D. dissertation, Southern Baptist Theological Seminary, 1970), p. 33.

7. *Ibid.,* p. 34, quoted from a Barton report.

8. *Ibid.,* p. 44.

9. *Ibid.,* p. 50.

10. *Ibid.,* p. 80.

11. *Ibid.,* p. 121.

12. Eighmy, *op. cit.,* p. 198.

13. *Ibid.,* p. 199.

14. The full pamphlet, which contains a like amount of material on "Basic Concepts Related to Social Principles," is available from the Christian Life Commission of the Southern Baptist Convention, 460 James Robertson Parkway, Nashville, Tennessee, 37209. Single copies free; quantity prices available on request. Other pamphlets on specific issues are available likewise.

afterword

Middle age invites introspection and critical judgments. Two of us were indulging in criticism of current trends in Southern Baptist life. Suddenly we returned to a measure of optimism when one of us observed, "But Southern Baptists couldn't be all bad. After all, they produced you and me."

Alex Haley in *Roots* has made us all more aware of the strengths and weaknesses of our differing heritages. With this sense both of debt and limitation I have tried to write of the faith and life of that portion of the People of God who are my heritage. It has necessarily been a witness from an insider. As such it could not be otherwise than an apologetic, even *apologia pro vita mea.* It is hoped that whatever of polemic has crept in at times has been in the spirit of love and justice. Certainly it is true that this witness is incomplete. The range and variety of Southern Baptist life demands the hearing of many diverse witnesses, even of other insiders. Most of all this human evaluation awaits the critical witness of non-Baptists who have come close enough to have been both blessed and cursed by our community of "saints with tarnished halos." To this end the author hopes that the current dialogues of the past ten years will inspire both a Roman Catholic and an Orthodox critical witness of Southern Baptists.

We can no longer ignore each other. Each of us has arrived as powerful Christian forces in American Christianity today. As the largest Protestant denomination, Southern Baptists have a stewardship toward both the secular world and the other Christian communions around us that we cannot deny. These two worlds no longer are impressed with our self-gratulatory poses as we progress on the ladder of religious success. They are demanding "zero-based budgeting" of our programs, our resources, even our purposes and goals in today's desperate world.

What then can Southern Baptists contribute? As long as religious liberty is still so fragile in many emerging nations and unrealized in many others, the leaven of Baptist ideals will be needed. In the light of much emphasis of the ecumenical movements on doctrinal and liturgical agreement, Baptists can contribute their own center of unity upon evangelism and missions. In the hunger of many Christians today for an experienced faith that brings joy and power into daily living, Baptists can contribute their dedication to the preaching and teaching of the Scriptures as a strong counterbalance to undisciplined emotionalism. In the rush toward security of person, of tribe, and of nation, if Baptists are true to the highest concept of "the security of the believer," they can point the way both to inner peace and liberation to seek freedom and justice for others.

In the developing respect for the dignity and power of the laity in the Church across many denominational lines, Baptists can contribute their reliance upon moral leadership based on persuasion and not merely upon office. The use of the laity in Bible teaching, "witnessing" and shared ministries can produce mature Christians who are becoming free from dependence upon authorities and free to undertake larger responsibilities as servants to justice and righteousness in the affairs of society and nations.

There are some congenital weaknesses of Baptists that hopefully can be overcome by becoming more deeply involved with other churches. Our success in becoming the largest Protestant denomination in America is perhaps our greatest snare. The danger is always there of concluding that "the Kingdom of God is up to us." Outsiders have already pointed out that just at the time Roman Catholics were officially abandoning "triumphalism" at Vatican II, Southern Baptists were picking it up. Often by the noises we make in our meetings, others conclude that we think only we are God's chosen of this generation. We can become so busy with our own programs that we can conveniently overlook, if not deny, our fellow Christians with whom the Lord is just as involved.

With our high sense of the autonomy of the local church another snare is to lose sight of our obvious interdependence with churches within the denomination. On the other hand, it is possible while boasting of that autonomy to lose it by an uncritical subservience to the "powers that be" in an ever-expanding denominational structure.

In the post World War II era Southern Baptists have risen on the socio-economic ladder to the point that we are in danger of losing our concern for the poor, the marginal peoples. There used to be a cliché that when Baptists in the county seat entered the managerial class, they joined the Presbyterians, and when they became owners, they sought out the Episcopalians. Affluence, however, has not only destroyed that but also the illusion that we are a poor and persecuted minority. Furthermore, in much of the South and Southwest Baptists can no longer blame any other power structure than themselves in the affairs of politics and civic righteousness. One other toll affluence exacts is the snare of believing that simply by giving money churches can discharge their obligations to minister sacrificially and fight courageously in a broken and unjust world.

On the ecumenical front, it ought to be apparent from the chapters above that Southern Baptists will probably never accept the goal of unity in one individual, institutional church. Even a papacy modified along the lines of servanthood and "the first among equals" would never be widely accepted. There would always be the demand of freedom and the question, "first among which equals?"

We applaud and hope to contribute to every worthy spiritual movement that enables us to rise above our ancient walls of separation. If both Baptists and others can learn to appreciate each other's heritage and to harmonize, not our differences, but our peculiar contributions, then we may confidently hope for progress in the Kingdom of God.

To that end this book is dedicated and sent out with the prayer that we may realize together the goal expressed by the Apostle Paul: "And so we shall all come together to that oneness in our faith and in our knowledge of the Son of God; we shall become mature men, reaching to the very height of Christ's full stature. . . . By speaking the truth in love, we must grow up in every way to Christ, who is the head. Under his control all the different parts of the body fit together, and the whole body is held together by every joint with which it is provided" (Eph. 4:13, 15–16, TEV).

appendix one

Excerpt from "A Statement of Social Principles for Christian Social Concern and Christian Social Action" by The Christian Life Commission, 1979

1. *Family Life.* The family, *God's first* and most basic *institution,* was written into our natures when he created us male and female. Created in the image of God, *husbands and wives* are partners with distinctive and supplemental roles to fulfill or functions to perform. Their relations with one another should be such that they are appropriately compared to the relation of Christ and his church. There should be a mutuality in their relationship, a mutual respect and sharing with one another, including their most intimate relationship—sexual union. *Parents* should love, teach and train, and properly discipline their *children,* bringing them up "in the discipline and instruction of the Lord." In turn, children should respect, honor, and obey their parents, although there may come a time in the lives of maturing children when they should obey God rather than their parents. Mature children should see that needy parents are properly cared for. It is difficult to know the proper interpretation of some scriptures regarding *divorce,* but it is clear that divorce is out of harmony with the fundamental purpose of God. His purpose is for one man and one woman to be joined together as husband and wife for life. Divorce, in the contemporary period, may seem at times to be the lesser-of-two evils but it should not be defended as something good within itself. Neither should it be treated as

the unforgivable sin. Churches should not only minister to the divorced but also provide an effective prevention program by preparing young people for marriage and by promoting family enrichment opportunities for the married. *Sex* is a gift of God and is good. However, the only full expression of it that God approves is the sexual union of husband and wife. This means that premarital and extramarital sex, homosexuality, and "open" or common-law marriages are out of harmony with the purposes of God. A contemporary issue that requires attention is the place of *women* both in society and in the churches. Women who need or choose to work outside the home should not be discriminated against while women who prefer not to work outside the home should be equally respected. Women should have an effective voice in the program and leadership of churches. The place of women in the structure of the churches, including ordination, in accordance with Baptist ecclesiology, is left to each local congregation.

2. *Race Relations.* There lingers among many people the entirely fallacious idea, sometimes referred to as *racism,* that some races are by nature inferior while others are superior. God, however, has made not innately inferior or superior races. All races have been created in the image of God. All belong to one family. This means that *racial prejudice* is to have no place in the life of a Christian or a Christian church. Our heavenly Father is no respecter of persons, and his children should not be. We are "all one in Christ Jesus." If we cannot pray "Our Father" with fellow believers of different colors and cultures, there is something wrong with our relation to their Father and our Father. Human distinctions such as male and female, white or black are transcended in him. He will break down the walls of prejudice that separate us if we will let him. A church that is "the church of God" cannot close its doors or its membership to anyone because of his or her race. Christians and churches are obligated to do what they can to eliminate expressions of prejudice in *housing* and in *jobs.* Housing is one of the most basic but difficult problems in the whole area of race relations. Many other problems stem from or are related to housing. Also, we should do what we can to prohibit discrimination in employment or discrimination regarding upgrading on the job on the basis of race. The ideal, in the area of *education,* should be that every child, regardless

of his racial origin, would have an opportunity for the best possible education. Every individual should have an opportunity to receive adequate education helpful to him in his chosen vocation.

3. *Economic Life and Daily Work.* There is no Christian *economic system.* The main concern of Christians should be what a system does for and to people. A Christian's daily work should enable him to find personal fulfillment, to provide for personal and family needs, and to give through his church to the cause of Christ around the world. *Profits* and the *profit motive* are not necessarily evil, but they should be kept subservient to service and the service motive. Human values are more important than material values. *Unemployment* and *underemployment* (part-time jobs or employment beneath the level of ability and training) are particularly persistent in democratic, industrialized countries. The Christian ideal is that every employable person should be able to secure employment suitable to his ability and training. *Poverty* and the relief of poverty have been a continuing concern of Christians. Christians are to have compassion for the poor so as to share with the needy in the local church family and with the poor in general. Government should be supported in providing an equitable *welfare system* that not only enables the employable to support themselves and their families but also enables the unemployable to maintain personal dignity. The restlessness of the poor is a major factor in the contemporary *world revolution* and the rise of the Third World; and the whole enterprise of missions is affected by how Christians perceive these poor and respond to their legitimate needs. Individual Christians and church and denominational agencies and organizations should seek to conserve energy, recognizing that the *energy crisis* is critical and will be with us for the foreseeable future. Many of us as believers should adopt a simpler *life style,* spending less on ourselves and sharing more with our church and the needy people of the world.

4. *Citizenship. Government* as an institution is *ordained* of God and derives its authority and its purpose from him. Christians should be law-abiding citizens and should respect and pray for those in authority. Also, they should use the ballot responsibly and should actively participate in the political process. Churches should pay taxes at the very least on any and all property except that used directly for worship and education. De-

nominational agencies should pay taxes on property that is competitive with legitimate business. Baptists should study and understand and propagate the principle of *religious liberty* and its immensely important corollary, *separation of church and state*. Baptists should not accept government funds for our agencies and institutions except possibly for very clear cases of specific contractual "services rendered."

Sectarian use of the *public schools* should be avoided. Also, Christians should be sensitive to the threat of a *civil religion* that tends to equate our national way of life or the culture of a particular region or group with the kingdom of God. As Christians we should be concerned about *war and peace*. Our aim should be peace and not war. We should do "the things which make for peace." Some military preparedness may be deemed necessary; but it should be kept under careful citizen scrutiny and civilian control. *Nuclear proliferation,* the multiplying of instruments of death and mass destruction, should be avoided through the concerned and active involvement of Christian citizens. Baptists, if consistent, will defend the right of the *conscientious objector* to war, even the selective conscientious objector. Basic to the biblical ideal of citizenship is the idea of *democracy* which magnifies the worth and dignity of the individual person. In contrast *totalitarianism* or statism or unrestrained nationalism considers the individual an instrument, whose worth is to be judged by his contribution to the program of the party or state. *Democracies,* religious or political, in contrast to totalitarian regimes, operate as open societies. The effective operation of a political democracy is dependent on a relatively strong democratic Christian movement. We are in the midst of a *world revolution* of major proportions. Christians should be sympathetic with the restless multitudes of the world, approving, in the main, their basic goals of freedom, self-determination, and fundamental *human rights* while disapproving some methods sometimes utilized in striving to attain those goals. *Civil disobedience* including acceptance of governmental punishment may sometimes be required, for Christians owe their ultimate allegiance not to government (Dan. 6:6–10) but to God (Acts 4:18–20).

5. *Special Moral Concerns.* On the basis of these and related principles, the *hunger* of any human being anywhere should be the concern of Christians everywhere, and efforts to relieve the

hunger of the world should include ways to increase production of food and to reduce its consumption in countries where over-consumption is a serious health problem, including the responsible limitation of population growth. We should also be concerned about crime and should work for a more enlightened and effective penal system where the emphasis is primarily remedial or custodial rather than merely punitive. There should be no place for *capital punishment* in a remedially oriented penal system because capital punishment is discriminatory in that most persons put to death are the very poor and the underprivileged from minority groups and because there is no clear evidence that capital punishment is a deterrent to crime. Christians should be deeply concerned about the lack of *integrity* in much of business, government, and society in general. *Law and order*, on the one hand, and *justice*, on the other, must be kept in proper balance if we are to have a healthy society. Christians should be careful not to become defenders of regimes that maintain order at the expense of justice for the people. *Freedom of the press* is constitutionally guaranteed in some countries; but there is no absolute freedom and no freedom without responsibility. Christians should support efforts to limit the publication and distribution of pornographic literature and the flagrant portrayal of *sex, violence, alcohol abuse*, and *materialism* in television programming. *Pollution* of water and air is a problem of major proportions in our society. Also, total abstinence from *gambling, smoking*, and *alcohol* and other harmful *drugs* is a preferable position for a Christian in our culture today. On the other hand, Christians should have a concern and compassion for the victims of these and other destructive habits. Some of the most pressing and perplexing moral problems in the contemporary world are in the *bio-medical* area. Among these are *abortion, euthanasia, organ transplants*, and *genetic engineering* and *experimentation*. There are moral as well as legal aspects of these problems. Christian doctors, scientists, and others should ask, "Is this right?" as well as "Is this legal?" One thing that will help in relation to many issues or cases will be a respect for life in general and human life in particular. In regard to abortion, euthanasia, and organ transplants, the decision at times is in the gray area when the choice may be between the lesser-of-two evils. Baptists generally believe, for example, that an abortion is justified only under very serious conditions: when there is a clear threat to the health or life of the mother or possibly in the case of a pregnancy as a result of incest or rape or manifest deformity of the fetus—cases that are extremely rare. It is important that the pregnant person should have competent Christian counseling with an opportunity to weigh her options, viewing abortion in moral and spiritual as well as physical terms. A distinction should be made between positive and negative euthanasia, with possible acceptance of the latter when it simply means the withholding of artificial means to keep a terminally ill person alive. In contrast, positive euthanasia, the actual taking of life, is wrong. Genetic engineering is potentially very dangerous. There is no reason to condemn organ transplants as long as there is proper regard for the donor as well as the recipient. Another moral issue is the *health,* including the mental health, of all the peoples of the world. The Christian ideal is that adequate medical service should be available to all.

A CHURCH COVENANT

This Covenant is one which has commonly been used by Southern Baptist churches in recent generations. It was written by J. Newton Brown and adopted by the Baptist Convention of New Hampshire in 1833 together with the widely used "New Hampshire Confession of Faith." The Covenant is not a creed, nor a statement of doctrinal beliefs, but a fellowship pledge by which members enter into Christian community and accept its disciplines. Each church is free to modify or write its own Covenant. In earlier years the Covenant was read at frequent intervals in the year and used as a basis of church discipline. Such use has presently greatly declined. However, one cannot understand Baptist polity apart from its covenantal nature (this is not to be confused with "covenantal theology" as taught by the Reformed churches and others).

Having been led, as we believe by the Spirit of God, to receive the Lord Jesus Christ as our Saviour, and on the profession of our faith, having been baptized in the name of the Father, and of the Son, and of the Holy Ghost, we do now, in the presence of God, angels, and this assembly, most solemnly and joyfully enter into covenant with one another, as one body in Christ.

We engage, therefore, by the aid of the Holy Spirit, to walk together in Christian love; to strive for the advancement of this church, in knowledge, holiness, and comfort; to promote its prosperity and spirituality; to sustain its worship, ordinances, discipline, and doctrines; to contribute cheerfully and regularly to the support of the ministry, the expenses of the church, the relief of the poor, and the spread of the gospel through all nations.

We also engage to maintain family and secret devotions; to religiously educate our children; to seek the salvation of our kindred and acquaintances; to walk circumspectly in the world; to be just in our dealings, faithful in our engagements, and exemplary in our deportment; to avoid all tattling, backbiting, and excessive anger; to abstain from the sale and use of intoxicating drinks as a beverage, and to be zealous in our efforts to advance the kingdom of our Saviour.

We further engage to watch over one another in brotherly love; to remember each other in prayer; to aid each other in sickness and distress; to cultivate Christian sympathy in feeling and courtesy in speech; to be slow to take offense, but always ready for reconciliation, and mindful of the rules of our Saviour to secure it without delay.

We moreover engage that when we remove from this place we will, as soon as possible, unite with some other church, where we can carry out the spirit of this covenant and the principles of God's Word.

GLOSSARY OF TERMS

ALIEN IMMERSION: a term, not so commonly used today, for the acceptance by the church of a member who was immersed after confession of faith by other than a Baptist church.

ANABAPTISTS: during the Reformation any of several groups who insisted on "rebaptizing" believers on the basis of "believer's baptism" only. They are spiritual forebears, but not organizationally linked with the later Baptists. Their descendants today are Mennonites.

ASSOCIATION: the first level of cooperation among Baptist churches in relatively small geographical regions (such as a county in areas with large Baptist population).

BABY DEDICATION: the practice of some Baptist churches of having a special service of dedicating parents and new babies to the Lord. It does not equal infant baptism, but it does pledge the parents to "raise their children in the nurture and admonition of the Lord."

BE CONVERTED: to experience salvation in Christ when one is "turned to Jesus" by the convicting power of the Holy Spirit using the Word of God and the testimony/preaching of Christians.

BE SAVED: to experience the beginning of the Christian life in the New Birth, accompanied by a sense of the forgiveness of sin, the love of Christ, and "love for the brethren."

BELIEVER'S BAPTISM: baptism administered only to those

who have made public profession of faith in Christ and requested baptism for themselves.

CHURCH COVENANT: a formal agreement of loyalty and support of the local congregation and its ministries, adopted at the organizational meeting of a new church.

CLOSED COMMUNION: the restricting of giving communion only to those who are members of the local congregation.

COMPETENCY OF THE SOUL: every human being is endowed by the Creator with the inalienable right and capacity to deal directly with God in all matters of religious faith and practice.

A CONFESSION OF FAITH: a statement of beliefs and practices drawn up by a church or association of churches for the purpose of identifying the doctrinal stance of that particular group of Baptists at that stated time.

COOPERATIVE PROGRAM: the plan adopted in 1925 by the Southern Baptist Convention (and entered into later by state conventions) by which all of the missions, educational and benevolent programs are supported through a unified budget. The Cooperative Program does not include the Sunday School Board, which supports itself and provides field services through its publishing business.

DISPENSATIONALISM: a system of interpretation of the Scriptures which divides human history into seven "ages" or periods, during which God tests mankind under differing "covenants."

EXPERIENCE OF GRACE: one's public testimony of how he became a Christian; most often used of candidates for ordination.

GENERAL BAPTISTS: those who hold to the "general" view of the Atonement of Christ, i.e., that Christ's offer of salvation is available to all mankind, and its acceptance is a matter of the free will of each individual. (This is not to be confused with the Free Will Baptists, who also teach that a saved person can be lost through grievious, unrepented sin.)

GROWTH IN GRACE: the development after "being saved": the continuing work of God's salvation that enables the believer's new life in union with Christ to develop through the grace of God. This grace operates through prayer, Bible study, ministering to others, "witnessing," worship and mutual support by other Christians. This progress in Christian maturity is a matter of individual desire and community support by the church.

HYPER-CALVINISTS: those followers (not necessarily Baptist) of the Reformer, John Calvin, who took his teachings to the logical conclusions of predestination, that is, that every person in the world is "chosen" by God in advance either for salvation or damnation.

JOIN THE CHURCH BY STATEMENT: to present oneself for membership in a local congregation on one's statement that he/she has been at one time a baptized member of a Baptist church, whose records are no longer available to provide "a church letter."

LANDMARKISM: a movement begun in the nineteenth century among Baptists that among other tenets holds that Baptists constitute the only true Church and that there exists a baptismal succession all the way back to the New Testament churches.

LICENSE TO PREACH: a letter of commendation to churches "of like faith and order" commending a new candidate for the ministry. This is preliminary to ordination, which must be called for by some particular local church.

MAKE CONFESSION OF FAITH—MAKE PROFESSION OF FAITH: usually at the close of a preaching service during the singing of a hymn of invitation to present oneself to the minister before the congregation proclaiming one's repentance and faith and (usually) requesting baptism and full membership in the local congregation. Sometimes the terms are used when the confession is made privately or in a group apart from a service in the church.

MESSENGERS to an Association/Convention: these are members elected by a local church to "sit" at the Association or

Convention annual meeting. Since the local church retains its full autonomy, "messengers" are not "delegates" to represent the will of the congregation, nor can they bind the latter by any vote of the annual meeting.

MILLENNIUM/MILLENARIAN: one who believes that at the second coming of Christ a thousand year period of peace under the rule of Christ will take place on earth (This is the "premillennial" view. Others hold that the millennium is either a symbol for the whole era between the first and second comings of Christ—"amillennialism"—or that Christ will come at the end of the thousand year period—"postmillennialism").

MOVE ONE'S MEMBERSHIP: "join the church by letter": to change affiliation with a local congregation upon a (standard) letter of recommendation from the former congregation that the member is in "good standing," i.e., not subject to discipline or expulsion.

ORDINANCE: term used of baptism and the Lord's Supper rather than "sacrament." These are the only two religious rites Baptists hold that Jesus "ordered" to be practiced in perpetuity by the Church.

PARTICULAR BAPTISTS: those who hold to the "particular" view of the atonement of Christ, i.e., that only those will be saved who are predestined by God unto salvation. This is usually associated with "irresistible grace" and thus denies the role of the human will in salvation. Southern Baptists, generally known as "modified Calvinists," believe that God "elects" people unto salvation by taking the initiative toward them, but that such election is not irresistible. Since it must be a matter of response by the human will, Southern Baptists believe in evangelism and missions (as over against "primitive Baptist Churches").

POLITY: the way in which a church or denomination structures its organization and carries out its practice. Historically the three most common polities are: hierarchical (Roman Catholic, Orthodox, Anglican), presbyterial (Presbyterian churches), and congregational (Baptist, United Church of Christ, Disciples of Christ).

PRESBYTERY: the group of pastors and deacons who are invited by a local congregation to examine a candidate for ordination and make recommendation to the church concerning the wisdom of ordaining such a person.

REGENERATION: the new birth engendered by the Holy Spirit whenever a sinner repents of sin toward God and commits himself/herself in faith to Jesus as Savior and Lord.

SECURITY OF THE BELIEVER: the assurance given by the Word of God and the inner witness of the Holy Spirit (Rom. 8:16) that salvation is fully guaranteed by the gift of God and cannot be lost short of actual renunciation of Jesus as Savior and Lord.

SEPARATISTS: English believers following the Reformation who became dissatisfied with the doctrines and practices of the established Church (Anglican). They included the Puritans, Baptists, and other congregational groups.

SOUL-WINNING/WITNESSING: telling others how to be saved, usually including how one became a Christian. Most often done by one or two with one who is not yet a believer.

UNSAVED/UNREGENERATE: those who have never been "born again" whether or not they have membership in any church or denomination.

COMMON QUESTIONS

In a ten-year effort of seeking to interpret Roman Catholics and Southern Baptists to each other, many questions by the former keep coming up. Instead of the usual topical Index, the following is offered as a guide to finding answers to the most common questions in the body of this book. Since we are referring solely to Southern Baptists, the words "Baptist" and "Baptists" will be taken for granted. *(Answer key is on page 153.)*

AUTHORITY

1. Why do they not have authorities to interpret the Bible for them?
2. What is meant by "local church autonomy"?
3. How do they know what is right or wrong?
4. How is the Bible used as authority for the individual?

BAPTISM AND LORD'S SUPPER

5. Why do they reject infant baptism?
6. Why do churches "rebaptize" those joining from other denominations?
7. Why do they not anoint the sick?
8. Why do they object to the word "sacrament"?
9. Why do they insist on baptism *after* a profession of faith?
10. Why do they baptize by immersion only?
11. Why is baptism publicly performed before the congregation?
12. Why are some baptized more than once?
13. Why do they not accept literally "This is my body"?

14. How do they celebrate the Eucharist?
15. How is Christ present in the Supper?
16. How often do they observe the Supper?

THE CHURCH

17. What is the "church"?
18. How does democracy operate in their churches?
19. How is a new church organized?
20. How is dissent handled?

ECUMENISM

21. Do they believe in the "Church universal"?
22. What is their attitude toward the ecumenical movement?
23. In what ways do they cooperate with other Christian bodies?
24. Why are they opposed to a U.S. representative to the Vatican?

MINISTRY

25. Why do they not have priests?
26. What authority does a pastor have?
27. What is "a call to preach"?
28. Do they insist on a married clergy?
29. How is a minister ordained?
30. How does a church get a new pastor?
31. What do deacons do?
32. How are lay people used in the church?

SALVATION

33. What role do "good works" have in salvation?
34. What does it mean to be "born again"?
35. Why do they claim "once saved, always saved"?
36. What about children who die before they are converted?
37. Why do Baptists seem to be concerned only with "getting saved" or the beginning of the Christian life?

SOCIAL CONCERNS

38. Why are they opposed to social drinking?
39. Why are they opposed to governmental aid to education?
40. What has been their stand on the Supreme Court's decision on desegregation of schools?

WORSHIP AND PRAYER

41. Why do they not pray to Mary and the Saints?
42. What happens in a typical worship service?
43. What is the role of singing in worship?

Answers

1. pg. 22	15. pg. 64	30. pg. 49
2. pgs. 11, 94	16. pg. 70	31. pgs. 49–51
3. pgs. 5–6	17. pgs. 7–8, 39–40	32. pg. 51
4. pgs. 13–14, 22–23	18. pg. 43	33. pg. 29
5. pgs. 13–14	19. pgs. 39, 42–43	34. pgs. 28, 30–31
6. pgs. 41, 61	20. pg. 100	35. pg. 34
7. pgs. 56–57	21. pgs. 51, 53, 88	36. pg. 33
8. pg. 65	22. pg. 97	37. pgs. 33–34
9. pg. 57	23. pgs. 97–100	38. pg. 102
10. pg. 60	24. pg. 100	39. pg. 117
11. pg. 61	25. pg. 19	40. pg. 130
12. pg. 61	26. pgs. 46–49	41. pgs. 71–74
13. pg. 65	27. pg. 47	42. pg. 73
14. pg. 63	28. pg. 47	43. pg. 73
	29. pg. 48	

bibliography

CHAPTER 1

Advanced Bible Study, April-May-June, 1971. The Sunday School Board of the Southern Baptist Convention, 1971.

Allen, Clifton J., ed., *The Broadman Bible Commentary,* Volume 1. Nashville: Broadman Press, 1969.

Angell, J. William, ed., *Catholics and Baptists in Ecumenical Dialogue.* The Ecumenical Institute of Wake Forest University, 1973.

The Baptist Faith and Message, Article VI, adopted by the Southern Baptist Convention, 1963.

Broach, Claude U., *The Baptists,* New York: Paulist Press, 1967.

Moody, Dale, "Authority," *Encyclopedia of Southern Baptists,* I. Nashville: Broadman Press, 1958.

Lumpkin, W. L., *Baptist Confessions of Faith.* Philadelphia: The Judson Press, 1959.

Mullins, E.Y., *Freedom and Authority of Religion.* Philadelphia: The Griffith and Rowland Press, 1913.

Wamble, Hugh, *Baptists, the Bible and Authority.* Foundations, July 1963.

CHAPTER 2

Armstrong, O. K. and Marjorie M., *The Indomitable Baptists.* New York: Doubleday and Company, 1967.

Baptist Ideals. Nashville: The Sunday School Board, SBC.

Mullins, E. Y., *The Axioms of Religion.* Philadelphia: American Baptist Publication Society, 1908.

Nordenhaug, Josef, "Baptists and a Regenerate Church Membership," *The Review and Expositor,* Volume LX, No. 2, Spring, 1963.

CHAPTER 3

Hays, Brooks and Steely, John E., *The Baptist Way of Life.* Prentice-Hall, 1963.

Ridderbos, Herman, *Paul, an Outline of His Theology.* Grand Rapids: Eerdmans, 1975.

CHAPTER 4

Baptist Confessions of Faith, Lumpkin, W. L. See Part 1, Chapter 1.

Baptist Ideals. See Part 1, Chapter 2.

"Baptists and a Regenerate Church Membership," Nordenhaug, Josef. See Part 1, Chapter II.

Carver, William O., *The Glory of God in the Christian Calling.* Nashville: Broadman Press, 1949.

————, "Introduction," *What Is the Church?,* McCall, Duke K., ed. Nashville: Broadman Press, 1958.

Price, Theron D., "The Church," *Encyclopedia of Southern Baptists.* Nashville: Broadman Press, Volume 1, 1958.

Shedd, Russell P., *Man in Community.* Grand Rapids: Eerdmans, 1964.

CHAPTER 5

Barth, Karl, *The Teaching of the Church Regarding Baptism.* London: SCM Press, 1948.

Beasley-Murray, G. R., *Baptism Today and Tomorrow.* New York: Macmillan, 1966.

Bernards, Rabbi Solomon S., *The Living Heritage of Passover.* New York: Anti-Defamation League of B'nai B'rith.

McCall, Duke K., ed., "The New Testament Significance of the Lord's Supper," *What Is the Church?* Nashville: Broadman Press, 1958.

Rahner, Karl, *et al.,* eds. "Baptism," *Sacramentum Mundi, Volume 1.* New York: Herder & Herder, 1968.

————, "Sacraments," *Sacramentum Mundi,* Volume 5. New York: Herder & Herder, 1968.

CHAPTER 6

Baker, Robert A., *A Baptist Source Book.* Nashville: Broadman Press, 1966.

Estep, William R., *The Anabaptist Story.* Grand Rapids: Eerdmans, 1975.

Littell, Franklin H., *The Free Church.* Boston: Beacon Press, 1957.

Torbet, Robert G., *A History of the Baptists.* Valley Forge: The Judson Press. The revised edition, 1963.

CHAPTER 7

Potter, Burtt, Jr., *Baptists: the Passionate People.* Nashville: Broadman Press, 1973.

Ryland, Raymond O., *A Study in Ecumenical Isolation: The Southern Baptist Convention.* Unpublished Ph.D. dissertation Marquette University, 1969.

Sullivan, James L., *Rope of Sand with Strength of Steel.* Nashville: Convention Press, 1974.

Sweet, William Warren, *Religion on the American Frontier: The Baptists, 1783–1830.* New York: Henry Holt & Co., 1931.

————, *op. cit.,* "The Records of the Forks of Elkhorn Baptist Church, Kentucky, 1800–1820."

CHAPTER 8

Albornoz, A. F. Carrillo de, *The Basis of Religious Liberty.* New York: Association Press, 1963.

Bainton, Roland H., *The Travail of Religious Liberty.* Philadelphia: The Westminster Press, 1951.

Baker, Robert A., ed., *A Baptist Source Book.* Nashville: Broadman Press, 1966.

Bender, Harold S., *The Anabaptists and Religious Liberty in the Sixteenth Century.* Philadelphia: Fortress Press, 1970.

Carr, Warren, *Baptism, Conscience and Clue for the Church.* New York: Holt, Rinehart & Winston, 1964.

Cuninggim, Merrimon, *Freedom's Holy Light.* New York: Harper
& Brothers, 1955.

Duncan, Pope A., "Baptists and Other Denominations," *Baptist
Advance.* Nashville: Broadman Press, 1964.

The Indomitable Baptists, Armstrong, O. K. and Marjorie. See
Part 1, Chapter 2.

Miller, Glenn T., *Religious Liberty in America.* Philadelphia: The
Westminster Press, 1976.

Murray, John Courtney, S.J., ed., *Freedom and Man.* New York:
P. J. Kennedy & Sons, 1965.

———, *Religious Liberty: An End and a Beginning.* New York:
The Macmillan Co., 1966.

Pfeffer, Leo, *Church, State and Freedom.* Boston: Beacon Press,
1967.

Wogamon, Philip, *Protestant Faith and Religious Liberty.* Nashville: Abingdon Press, 1967.

CHAPTER 9

Gaddy, Curtis Welton, "The Christian Life Commission of the
Southern Baptist Convention: A Critical Evaluation," Un-
published Ph.D. dissertation, Southern Baptist Theological
Seminary, 1970.

Kelsey, George D., *Social Ethics Among Southern Baptists, 1917–
1969.* Metuchen, New Jersey: The Scarecrow Press, 1973.

Minutes of the Baptist General Association of Virginia, 1920.

Pinson, William M., Jr., *Applying the Gospel.* Nashville: Broadman Press, 1975.